Contents

NEW LOGO

A COLLECTION OF CORPORATE

IDENTITIES

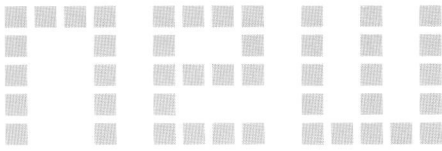

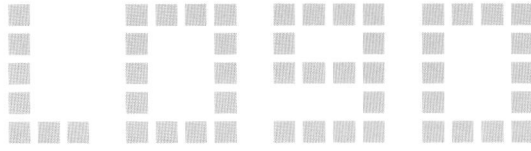

NEW LOGO A COLLECTION OF CORPORATE IDENTITIES
2004 © PAGE ONE PUBLISHING PRIVATE LIMITED

Published in 2004 by
Page One Publishing Private Limited
20 Kaki Bukit View
Kaki Bukit Techpark II
Singapore 415956
Tel: (65) 6742-2088
Fax: (65) 6744-2088
enquiries@pageonegroup.com
www.pageonegroup.com

Distributed by:
Page One Publishing Private Limited
20 Kakit Bukit View
Kaki Bukit Techpark II
Singapore 415956
Tel: (65) 6742-2088
Fax: (65) 6744-2088

2004 © Liaoning Science and Technology Publishing House
Printed by SNP LeeFung Printers (Shen Zhen) Co.,Ltd
Chief Editor: Chen Ci Liang
Cover Design: Kelley Cheng, Meng Xinxin
Compiled by: Zhou Jianzhong, Feng Bin
Translator: Zhao Minchao
Format Design: Yin Jie
Examiner: Kang Qian, Jiang Lu

ISBN: 981-245-122-6

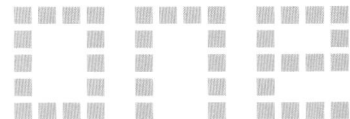

ONE

Printed in China

1
KANKYO DESIGN

2
HEENE

3
TIMBERLAND PRESSURE WASH

4
CELESTICA

5
PRECISION

6
KOREA HIGHWAY CONSTRUCTION &
SERVICE

7
RAINBOW FOSTERING SERVICES

1

4

5

2

6

3

7

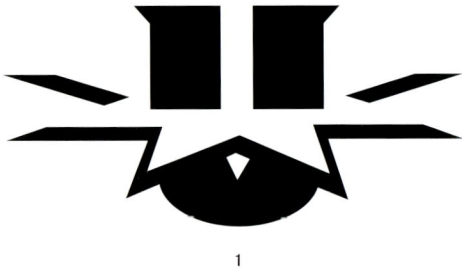

1

2

3

4

THE DRIVER PROVIDER

5

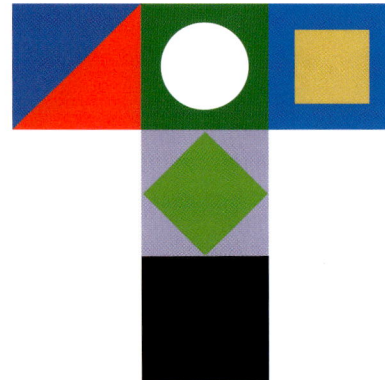

6

7

1
UNDERGROUND STORAGE

2
MOVELINE

3
FAIR ISAAC

4
MEDITECH BILLING & CONSULTING,
LLC

5
THE DRIVER PROVIDER

6
TOTALIZER AGENCY BOARD

7
BUDGET

1
DASSAULT

2
24 ASSISTANCE

3
BLUE MAN CLEANING

4
AUDIOS AMIGOS

5
DOLLAR RENT A CAR

6
ORION

7
INDUSTRIAL PLANT SERVICES

DASSAULT
FALCON JET

1

audios
AMIGO

4

DOLLAR
R E N T A C A R

5

24
Assistance

2

ORION
EARTH SERVICES CORP

6

bluemen
cleaning

3

7

7

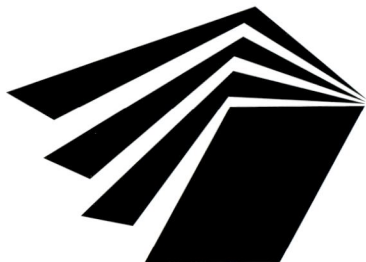

1

2

3

4

5

6

7

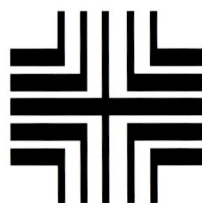

8

1
NEWSLETTER SERVICES INC.

2
RABBIT COPIER AND SERVICE

3
NEW YORK TV SHOW TICKETS

4
MAJESTIC LAUNDRY

5
PMSOLUTIONS

6
PANACHE RESOURCES & SYSTEMS CORP

7
CENTER CITY DISTRICT

8
PITNEY BOWES

CERPLEX

1

DISCOUNT™
CLEANERS

4

National®

5

2

6

GLADIATOR
GARAGEWORKS

3

BOWHAUS

7

MOSS CAIRNS

Raising meetings to new heights

1

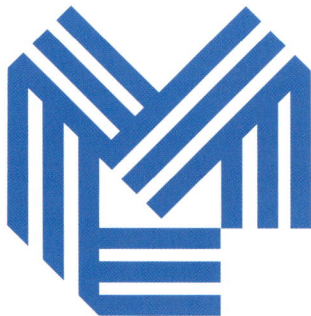

DAHIDO'S

5

kaunet
カウネット

2

BIG WASH

6

3

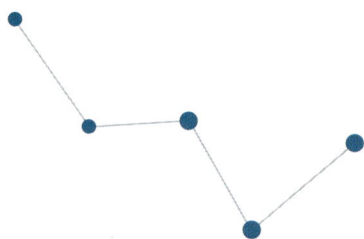

The Company Warehouse

7

StarContents

4

simple Clean

8

1
MOSS CAIRNS

2
KAUNET CO.LET

3
MERCANTILE LEASING CORP

4
STAR CONTENTS

5
DAHIDO'S CLEANING SERVICE

6
BIG WASH

7
THE COMPANY WAREHOUSE

8
SIMPLE CLEAN

1
TO DINE FOR INC

2
RC CUSTOM CLEAN

3
GLENN SOUND

4
COMDISCO

5
VANSTAR

6
SIMPLY CATERING

7
FLIGHT TIME

8
LINEDATA SERVICES

To Dine For Inc.
1

COMDISCO®
4

Vanstar
5

RC CUSTOM CLEAN
2

Simply Catering
6

FlightTime
7

REAL DOCTORS
3

LINEDATA SERVICES
8

N>D

NEURON DATA

1

Hertz

exactly.®

2

B O U L L I O U N

3

BIKE**PRO** MOBILE

4

Coop's

5

abs

A L A S K A

B I L L I N G

S E R V I C E S

6

EQUITY HOME
L E N D I N G

7

1
SAFETEMP

2
MOBILNET MANAGEMENT SERVIC-
ES.INC

3
SOUTH PARK STADIUM GROUP

4
THE DANCING CHEF

5
RESOURCE LINK

6
SERVICES INTEGRATION GROUP

7
STORE & LOCK

8
BMW PERFORMANCE CENTER

1

5

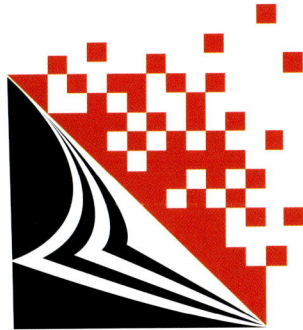

2

6

3

7

4

8

Pinal Gila COMMUNITY CHILD SERVICES, INC

1

2

JUST RECRUITMENT UK

3

Black River Canoe Rentals

4

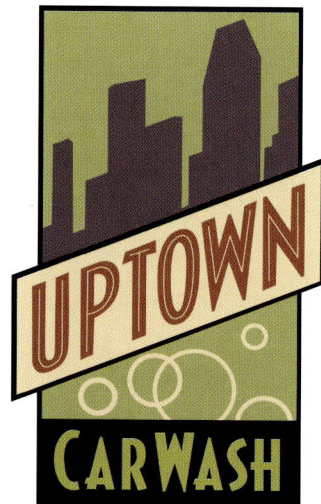

Keen Recruitment

5

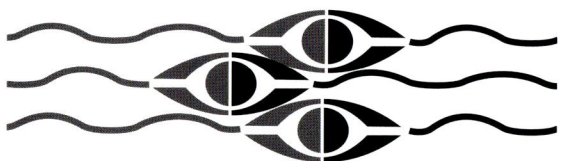

UPTOWN CarWash

6

News-Type Service, Inc.

7

1
PINAL GILA COMMUNITY CHILD
SERVICES, INC

2
LILY LANGTRY COACH COMPANY

3
JUST RECRUITMENT UK

4
BLACK RIVER CANOE RENTALS

5
KEEN RECRUITMENT

6
UPTOWN CAR WASH

7
NEWS TYPE SERVICE.INC

1
MEDIA LYNX INFORMATION SER-
VICES

2
ACCURTE TYPING SERVICES INC

3
ACCEL REALTY

4
ANTARES LEVERAGED CAPITAL

5
ORPORATE CONCEPTS-PARADIGM
BUSINESS SOLUTIONS

6
FEDDS

7
TIMESHARE DIRECT

8
WEDDINGNITE

1

5

2

6

3

7

4

8

15

JAL

1

2

3

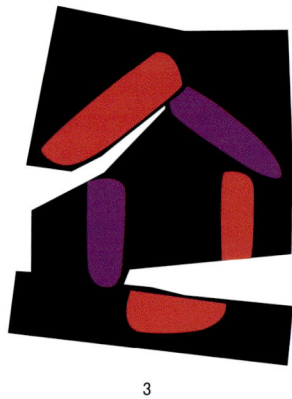

Eastport
BUSINESS CENTER

4

TARGET

5

6

TUSCAN
SQUARE

7

1
JAL

2
T Fresh

3
HAMILTON COURT

4
EASTPORT BUSINESS CENTER

5
TARGET

6
MELBOURNE TOWN CENTRE

7
TUSCAN SQUARE

1
UNIVERSITY MALL

2
THE PLAZA

3
BEST BUY

4
DONGAH DEPARTMENT STORE

5
DAYTON MALL

6
ALGARVE SHOPPING

7
SUMMER OAKS BUSINESS PARK

university mall

1

4

DAYTON MALL

5

THE **PLAZA**
RESTAURANTS · CINEMAS
AT THE PROMENADE

2

ALGARVE SHOPPING

6

BEST BUY®

3

Summer Oaks
BUSINESS PARK

7

1

5

2

3

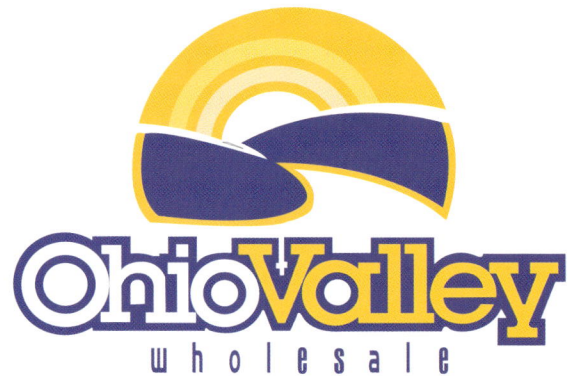

6

4

7

1
GEORGETOWN UNIMETAL SALES

2
ONLY

3
THE HOME DEPOT

4
PETCO

5
ASDA PRICE

6
FARGET

7
GLEN BURNIE MALL

1

2

3

4

5

6

7

19

1

2

3

4

CareDirect.com

5

PILAR

6

Baypoint Mall

7

1
SAM'S CLUB

2
APPLE VALLEY INTERATIONAL.INC

3
TURBO TOTS

4
APPLE DISTRIBUTORS

5
CARE DIRECT.COM

6
PILAR

7
BAYPOINT MALL

1
GARZA OPTICAL

2
KIRK ALFORD

3
CARLA'S CATS

4
HOLLAND

5
THE CAT

6
YURY'S PIANO

7
JOHN WILMER STUDIOWORKSHOP
ANTIQUE RESTORATION & UP-
HOLSTERY

8
TOURNEAU WATCH GEAR

1

THE CAT

5

2

6

Carla's Cats

3

7

Holland Photo

4

TOURNEAU
watch gear

8

21

1

3

2

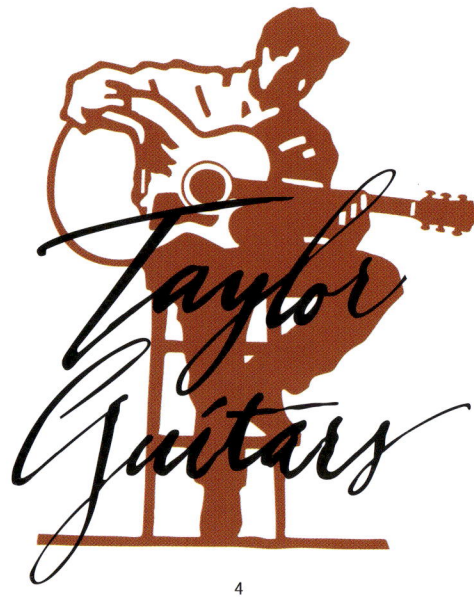

4

1
PHAROS OPTICS

2
FANCY KOI OUTLET

3
THE TREE HOUSE

4
THE SCOOTER STORE

5
LAND OF OZ

6
SAM'S CLUB

7
LITTLE PASSENGER SEATS

1

5

2

6

3

4

7

URBAN

1

4

5

2

6

3

7

1
CANDLE CRAFT

2
W Flower

3
HALL MARK

4
OCEAN VIEW GIFTS

5
YUM YUM CANDY AND GIFTS

6
ALYSSA BASKET DESIGNS

7
COLE MYER DIRET

8
ALL CLAD METALCRAFTERS LLC

1

5

2

6

3

7

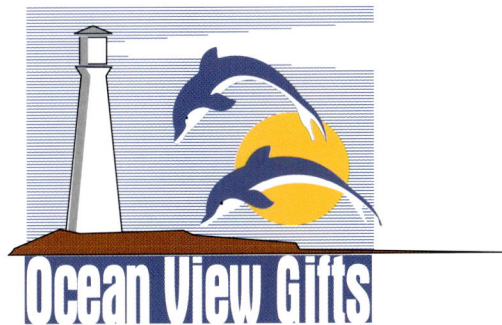

4

8

1

2

3

4

5

6

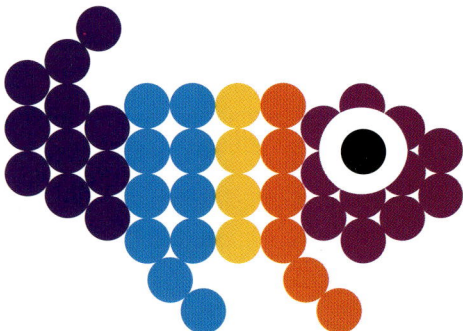

7

8

1
JOLI GIFTS

2
THURBER WORKS

3
KINGSLEY CARDS

4
CHAMELEON COLOR CRAFTS

5
SIRIHATI WEDDING CARDS

6
THE MANGO TREE OF NEW YORK

7
BON VOYAGE GIFT PACK

8
SOUL OF THE PLANT

1
LE CARE GIFT BASKETS

2
432

3
BALLYHOO

4
AMERICAN GREETINGS

5
GREETWAY

6
EGREETINGS.COM

7
FIESTA SOUTHWEST GIFTS

1

4

5

2

6

3

7

1
COOL BLAST

2
LOLO

3
TITO

4
BITTY BABY

5
PIGEON

6
GEAR UP

7
FUN 4 ONE

1

4

5

2

6

3

7

29

1

2

3

4

5

6

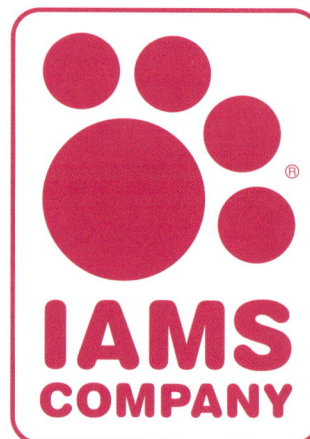

7

1
PRINCE

2
BIG IDEA

3
GIGO

4
PUKU.PETIT

5
SAFE KIDS

6
DOOBY

7
THE IAMS COMPANY

1
CHILDALERT

2
FIT FOR A KID

3
A STEP BEYOND

4
BABY SUPERSTAR

5
BABY JOGGER

6
DIE ECONAUTEN

7
MEGA BLOKS

4

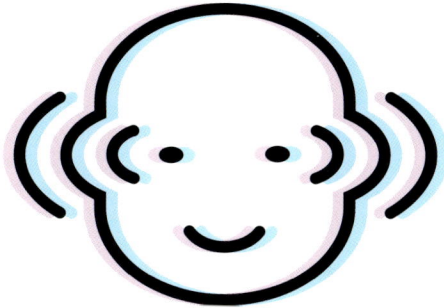

1

5

2

6

3

7

1

2

5

6

3

4

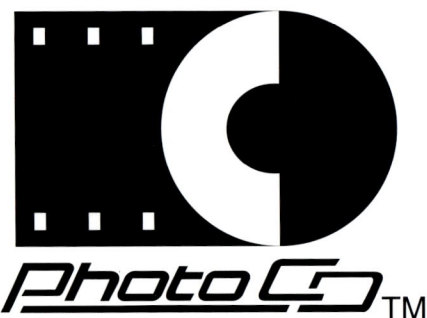

7

1
BEARCAT SCANNERS

2
COLORAD PRINTERS

3
LEXJET DIRECT

4
CIBA

5
INFOCUS

6
MEYER PROJECTION SYSTEMS

7
INFOCUS

8
PROJECTOR PEOPLE.COM

1

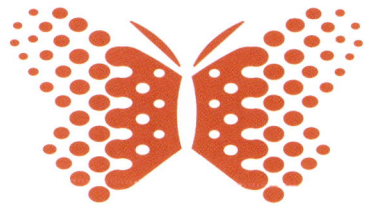

2

3

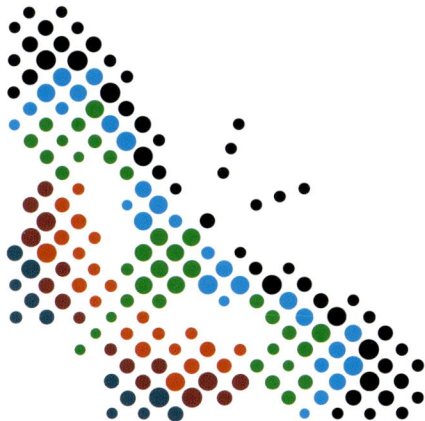

4

InFocus®
makes it easy.

5

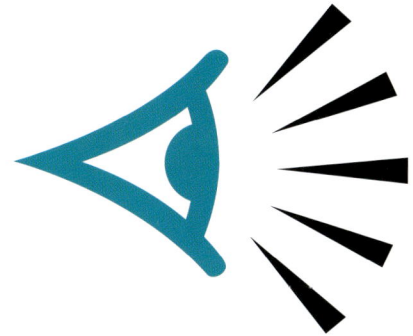

6

7

8

Plantin Soap

1

IVORY ®

5

STRIDEX ®

2

STAIN OUT

3

PULEVA

www.puleva.es

6

CELANESE

4

Pure & Natural

7

1
ALLSPORT CONCEPTS

2
NAD'S SQUEEGEE CREME HAIR R-
EMOVAL SYSTEM

3
DAWN

4
KOHLER

5
ARMOR ALL

6
BEST DEFENSE PROGRAM

7
KNIGHT'S PAINT AND WALLPAPER

ALLSPORT

CONCEPTS™

1

KOHLER®
COORDINATES™

4

ARMOR ALL™

5

Nad's
Squeegee
&Crème
Hair Removal System

2

Best Defense
PROGRAM

6

DAWN
SpecialCare

3

knight'spaint&wallpaper

7

35

1

2

3

4

5

6

7

1
MESA MICROWAVE INC

2
THE CELLAR

3
GOZO

4
CHEFWEAR

5
MINEING—KITCHENWARE&OUTDOOR
GOODS BRAND

6
LAPP'S KITCHEN. INC

7
U.S.A KNIFE

1
MISTY RIVER WOODWORKS

2
THE SCOUT GROUP

3
MOVING BUTTERFLIES.COM

4
SELECT COMFORT

5
INFINITE FISHING

6
RUSS

7
QUIET TIME

SELECT COMFORT®

4

1

5

2

6

3

7

PROMOSEDIA

1

ASPEN
HOME SYSTEMS

2

Benjamin Moore Paints

3

SUMMIT

4

A

5

DANISH DESIGN

6

RELAX THE BACK

7

1
PROMOSEDIA

2
ASPEN HOME SYSTEMS

3
BENJAMIN MOORE PAINTS

4
SUMMIT

5
ANDREW PAINT

6
DANISH DESIGN

7
RELAX THE BACK

Masonite International Corporation

4

1

5

DEVINE
PAINTERS

2

6

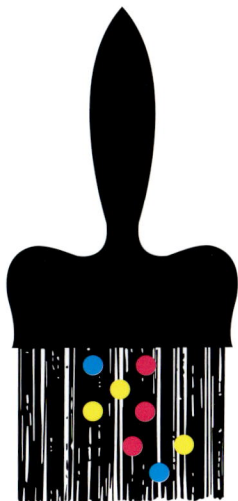

3

7

STILWELL PAINTING INC.

1

2

ANTHRO
TECHNOLOGY FURNITURE®

3

adatto

4

5

Pine Hill
Furniture

6

PIANETA
LEGNO

7

1
STILWELL PAINTING INC

2
MONTIS

3
ANTHRO TECHNOLOGY FURNITURE

4
ADATTO

5
NOSONG FURNITURE

6
PINE HILL FURNITURE

7
PIANETA LEGNO

1
ATELIER DES SOURDS.INC

2
PHYS.SCI.

3
PURPL BRIDGE

4
JBL

5
LIVE PICTURE

6
EML PLC

7
I-AUDIO

8
AUDIOVOX

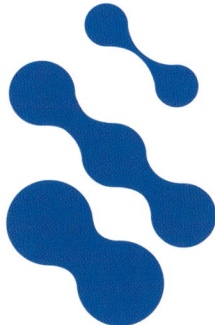

1

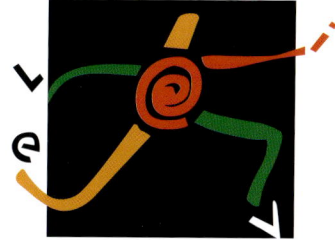

LIVE PiCTURE

5

PHYS.SCI.™

2

6

purpl bridge ™

3

i AUDIO

7

JBL

4

AUDIOVOX®

8

SHANGHAI 1930
RESTAURANT

1

chili's

2

LYN'S CAFE

3

S. ASIMAKOPOULOS

CAFE

4

1
GOC HOLDINGS INC

2
CHILIS

3
LYN'S CAFE

4
S.ASIMAKOPOULOS CAFE

5
CAFFE MARSEILLE

6
ITALIA RESTAURANT

7
CANDY

5

6

Candy Candy
DISCOTHEQUE RESTAURANT BAR

7

ZAKS

1

5

1
HYDRA CAFE

2
NEW YORK OFFICIAL ALL STAR-
CAFE

3
CARL'S CAFE

4
SILVANO

5
LE GOURMAND

6
WHITE CASTLE

7
GARDEN BURGER

2

6

3

4

7

44

1
BINKER

2
CONSOLIDATED CORRECTIONAL
FOOD

3
BIG BOWL ASIAN KITCHEN

4
CULINARY CONCEPTS

5
SPAR KLIPP

6
SUN+MOON

7
TONGA

1

4

5

2

6

3

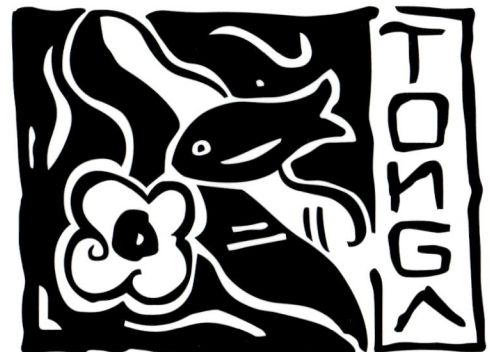

7

45

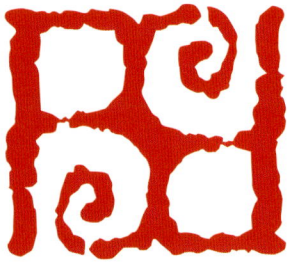

BRIOSO BRAZIL
an american churrascaria

1

2

BISTECCA

3

CAFE
LAZARUS

5

FOOD & FUN
FUN·JUNCTION
FOREVER!

6

4

POLO
RESTAURANT

7

1
MARKETPLACE GRILL

2
WHALE'S TALE SEAFOOD RESTAURANT

3
BISTECCA

4
SERGEANT'S

5
CAFE LAZARUS

6
FUN JUNCTION

7
POLO RESTAURANT

1
GREEN PEAS

2
IBOC INC

3
DASH RUSH

4
SCOTT'S SEAFOOD

5
CAFE PARAGON

6
ON THE GO COOKIES

7
CIBOLA

1

4

5

2

6

3

7

47

1

2

3

Excellence in Arabic Food

4

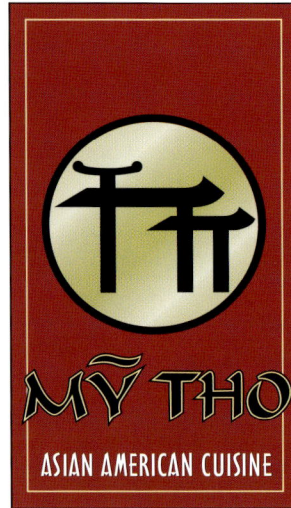

MỸ THO

ASIAN AMERICAN CUISINE

5

MILLENNIUM QUIZINE

CUISINE, A THOUSAND TIMES BETTER

6

7

1
PUMPERNICKEL'S CAFE & DELI

2
CORNER GOURMET

3
LA COCINA

4
AMIR

5
MY THO

6
MILLENNIUM QUIZINE

7
ENGFER PIZZA WORKS

1
ESPRESSO 2U

2
ESPRESSO 2U

3
ESPRESSO 2U

4
ESPRESSO 2U

5
ESPRESSO 2U

1

3

4

2

5

1

2

3

4

5

6

7

1
THE MARSH RESTAURANT

2
LA RAZA

3
CAFE LU LU

4
THE CORNELIA STREET CAFE

5
DANTE'S RESTAURANT.INC

6
THE PAMPERED CHEF

7
KAPLAN HAT CO.RESTAURANT

1
PICASONIC CAFE

2
JACKSON HOLE

3
NANNA'S SOUL FOOD CAFE

4
LAKESIDE CAFE

5
PORLOBELLO

6
PASTA BENE

7
RED TOMATO

1

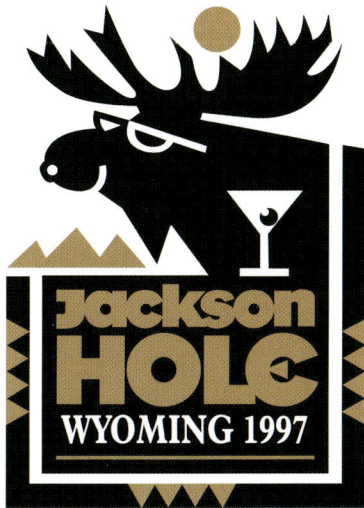

4

2

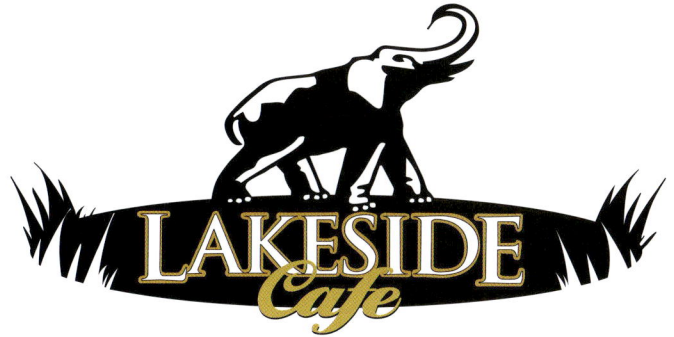

5

6

3

7

1

2

3

picnic
works

4

JUPITER'S
PIZZA · POOL

5

6

7

1
TWISTER CAFE

2
MONFALCONE RISTORANTE PIZZE-
RIA

3
STARLAND CAFE

4
PICNIC WORKS

5
JUPITER'S PIZZA & POOL

6
STOLI

7
CAFE A GO GO

1
TOSCANA

2
CHILLI'S

3
BASIL PROSPERI

4
JUNIORS MOST FABULOUS REST-
AURANT

5
IBERIA

6
CHESSBOARD CAFE

7
MIRACOLI

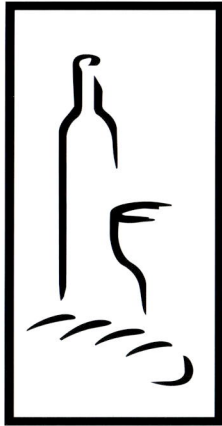

TOSCANA

1

5

2

ristorante

3

6

4

7

EUROPA
ESPRESSO BARS

1

5

1
EUROPA ESPRESSO BARS

2
COFFEE WAVE

3
MUGSY'S COFFEE HOUSE&CIGAR CO.

4
NEWCO

5
NETWORTH CAFE

6
CAFE LA

7
EXPERIENCE COFFEE

COFFEE WAVE

2

steam of consciousness

Mugsy's
COFFEE HOUSE & CIGAR CO.

3

café LA

6

NEWCO

4

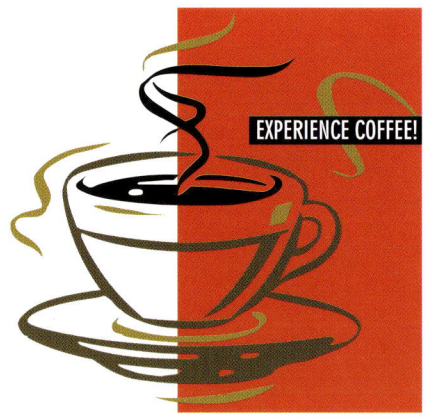

EXPERIENCE COFFEE!

7

54

1
CAFE ITALIA

2
VERLAINE

3
APPART LLC

4
GRACE ACADEMY

5
BESTSELLERS BOOKS TO BEANS

6
VILLAGE COFFEE

7
START

1

4

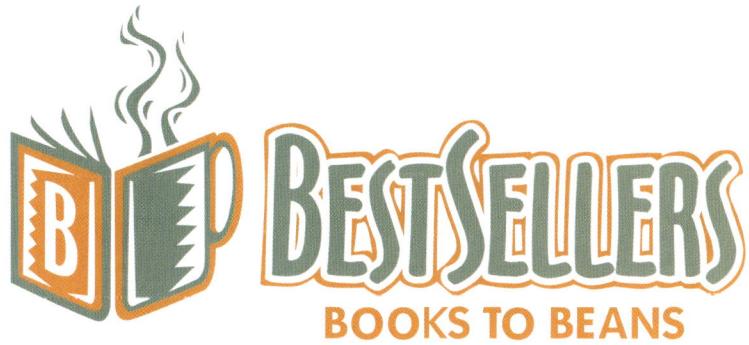

BESTSELLERS
BOOKS TO BEANS

5

2

VILLAGE
COFFEE COMPANY

6

APPART llc.

Greating that coffce house feeling

3

START

7

Z O ë

1

Z O ë

5

1
ZOE PAN-ASIAN CAFE

2
COURTYARD CAFE

3
VICTORY COFFEE

4
CASABLANCA CAFE

5
ZOE PAN-ASIAN CAFE

6
CITY COFFEE HOUSE

7
STARBUCKS COFFEE

C O U R T Y A R D

C A F E

2

3

CITY

coffeehouse

6

Casablanca
C A F E
ADDIS ABABA

4

Starbucks

7

1
PHILL IT TO THE BRIM

2
CUOCA CAFE

3
COFFEE HOUSE

4
TIRAMISU CAFE

5
CENTRAL PERK

6
BARI'S PIZZERIA & CAFE

7
MOUNTAIN BREW

1

4

5

2

6

3

7

1

5

2

6

3

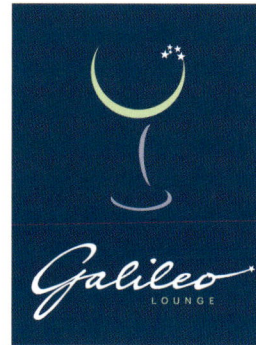

7

drinks. fun. seger.

4

8

1
CABANA RESTAURANT&BAR

2
PIZZAZZ SPORTS BAR

3
CLUB CAFE MOOSIS

4
BOB BAR

5
CHIPS

6
LOFT 150

7
GALILEO LOUNGE

8
THE LIZARD LOUNGE

1
HULLABALLOO

2
TAZO TEA

3
GREENWICHPIZZA

4
FAT CAT TEA COMPANY

5
THE WORLD MASTER OF CULINARY
ARTS

6
L'AMYX

7
RICCARDO'S PIZZA

1

5

2

6

3

4

7

1

2

3

4

5

6

7

1
COZYMEL'S COASTAL GRILL

2
STEAMER'S GRILLHOUSE

3
COWTOWN CATERING

4
BORDER GRILL

5
BILLY'S

6
ON THE BORDER MEXICAN GRALL
& CANTINA

7
ROCKFISH SEAFOOD GRILL

1
FIREHOWIE

2
TRUETT'S GRILL

3
CORNER BAKERY CAFE

4
CABO

5
MOUNTAIN DELL GRILL

6
ALKI

7
RUBIOS BAGA GRILL

8
ELI'S

1

5

2

6

3

7

4

8

61

1

Great
American
Food

5

2

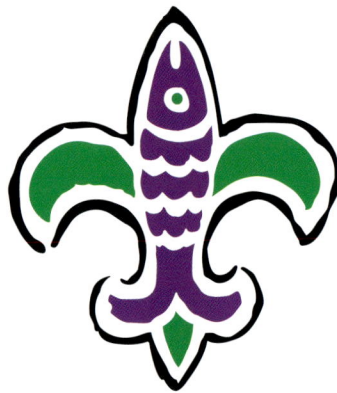

3

CURBSIDE TO GO

6

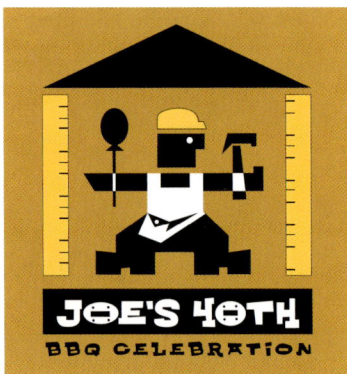

JOE'S 40TH
BBQ CELEBRATION

4

COYOTE GRILL

7

1
FOGODECHAD

2
WAHOO

3
SALTGRASS STEAK HOUSE

4
JOE'S 40TH BBQ CELEBRATION

5
GREAT AMERICAN FOOD—BAKERY

6
ROMANO'S MACARONI GRILL

7
COYOTE GRILL

1
STACKS

2
CHESAPEAKE BAGEL BAKERY

3
BELLAGIO BAKERY

4
KENYA'S GOURMET BAKERY

5
NATHAN'S SOUP AND SALAD

6
BAKERIES BY THE BAY

7
FIREKING BAKING CO.& BISTRO

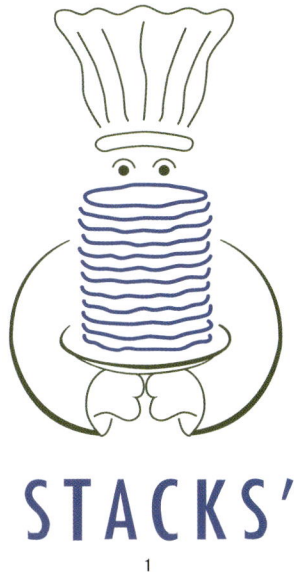

STACKS'

1

kenya's
GOURMET BAKERY

4

NATHAN'S
SOUP AND SALAD

5

Chesapeake
Bagel
Bakery

2

6

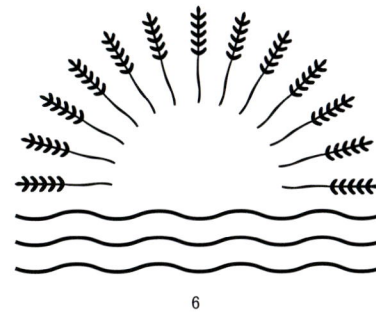

BELLAGIO
BAKERY

3

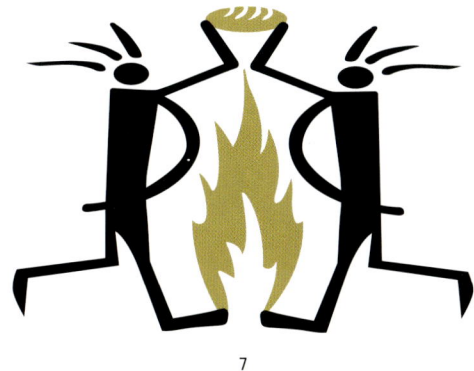

7

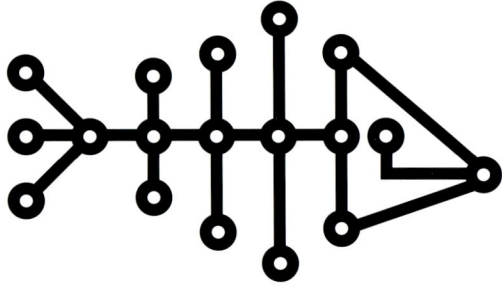

1

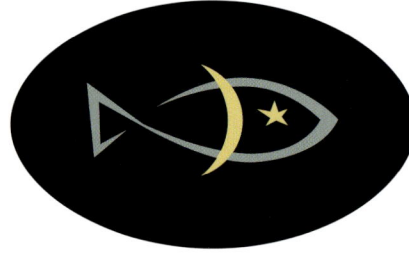

SUSHI GIRL

2

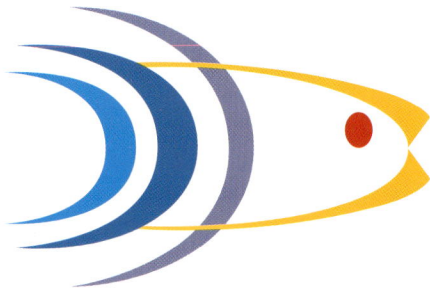

3

1
TEKNO SUSHIRESTAURANT

2
SUSHI GIRL

3
ASOY SUSHI

4
SUSHI NIGHT

5
FUNAS SUSHI BAR

6
NIPPON SUSHI

4

5

6

1
CALIFORNIA DRIED PLUMS

2
TREAT YOUR BODY

3
KOOL-AID

4
EXOULSITE TASTE AND TENDERN-
ESS MONTANA LEGEND NATURAL
ANGUS BEEF

5
PRODUCE ONE

6
GRUMA

7
ENRICH

1

5

2

3

6

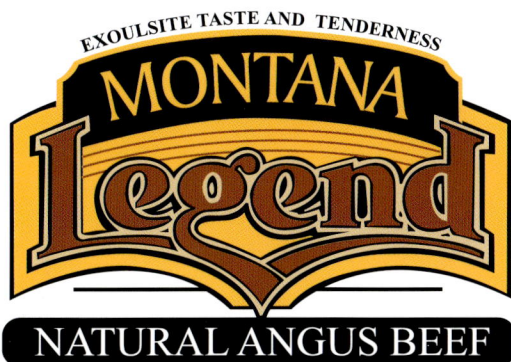

4

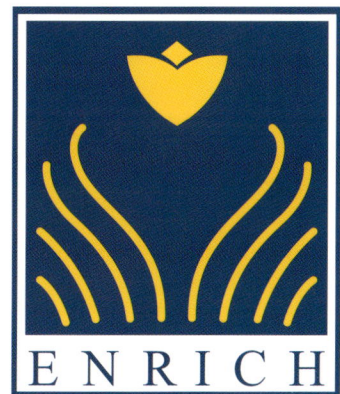

7

Coréana

1

Anergen

5

NATROL™

2

BODIES in BALANCE

6

CARTE NOIRE

3

Shaklee®
Creating Healthier Lives™

4

Roo's Snack Shack

7

1
NATURAL SELECTION FOODS

2
WASSERKRAFTWERK EGG

3
WINGS AND THINGS

4
CORNSILK

5
PUPPY LOVE BISCUITS

6
TALLGRASS BEEF

7
FATIGUE BUSTERS

3

5

4

6

1

2

7

1

2

5

6

3

4

7

1
PENINSULA FOODS

2
HOMEMADE

3
COTE D'OR

4
COOLAVA ISLANDS

5
ROMAN MEAL

6
WISE LIVING

1

4

2

5

3

6

1

SELECT
Health Products

5

PATiO

2

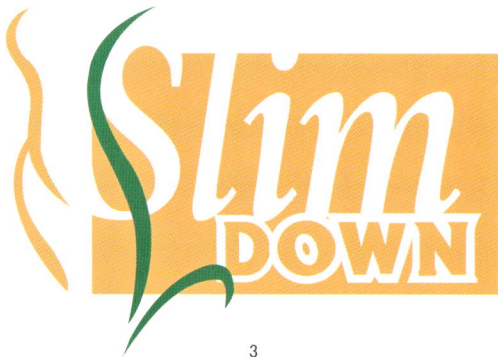

CHICKENVILLE

6

Slim DOWN

3

Cargill™

Nourishing Ideas. Nourishing People.™

4

Panera BREAD

7

1
PASKESZ

2
WILDFLOWER BREAD COMPANY

3
BLOOMING PRAIRIE NATURAL FO-
ODS

4
HORMEL

5
RED HOT PEPPER SAUCE

6
GENERAL MILLS

7
CAN PAN CANDY

4

1

5

2

6

3

7

1

2

3

4

5

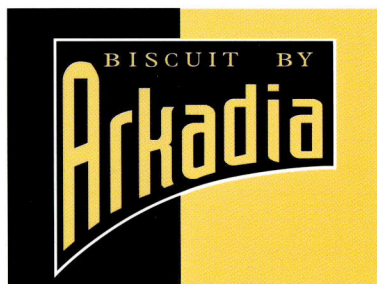

6

7

1
ALFA

2
WHIPPED TOPPING COOL WHIP

3
BAGEL HEAVEN

4
ARKADIA

5
TRISCUIT

6
BALANCE

7
LUNA THE WHOLE NUTRITION BAR
FOR WOMEN

1
KEY SABINAL

2
KELLER GROVES INC

3
THE HAYES CO

4
HOKUREN PET FOODS

5
BOW WOW BEAN

6
TOREHA

7
NATURAL INSTINCTS

3

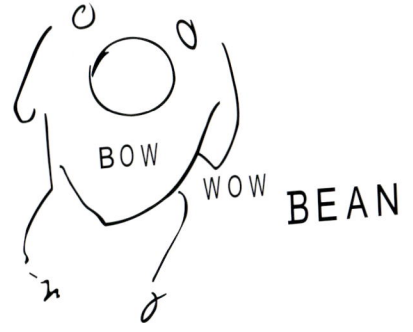

5

1

HOKUREN PET FOODS

4

6

Keller Groves, Inc.

2

7

1

2

3

4

5

6

1
JACOBS

2
ROWNTREE

3
FRISKIES

4
HERTA

5
CHAMBOURCY

6
MAGGI

1
SOUTHWEST GOURMET
FOOD SHOW

2
ONY/ORIGINAL NATURE YARD

3
CEORGIA ORGANICS

4
EAT 5 A DAY FOR BETTER HEAL-
TH

5
HEALTHY CHOICE

6
FIBERCOMM L.L.C

7
GEN SOY

SOUTHWEST GOURMET
FOOD SHOW

1

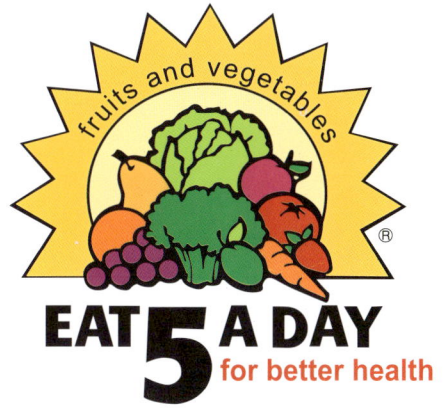

fruits and vegetables
EAT 5 A DAY
for better health

4

HEALTHY CHOICE

5

ony
original nature yard

2

FiberComm L.L.C.

6

GEORGIA
ORGANICS

3

GenSoy®
Soy That Tastes Good.

7

MINERAL SPRINGS

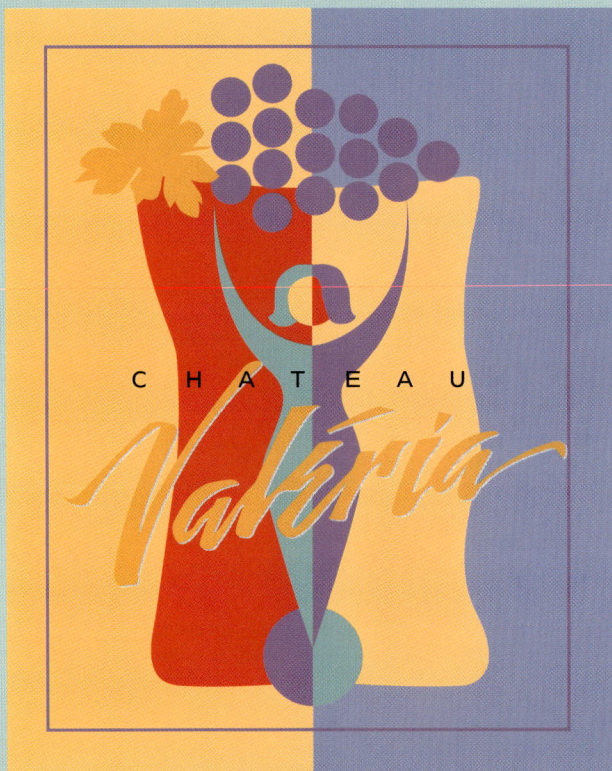

CHATEAU
Valéria

1
LIME DADDY

2
SNOW BALL

3
AQUAPENN SPRING WATER COMPANY

4
GELATI MOTTA

5
NATIVE PLANET

6
KENCO

7
7UP

1

5

2

6

3

4

7

1

5

NextGen
2

CROSSE & BLACKWELL
3

6

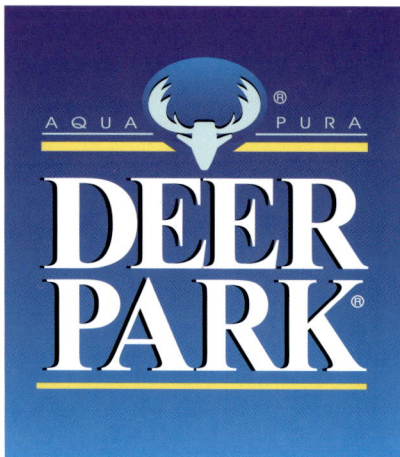
AQUA PURA
DEER PARK
4

MINERAL SPRING
7

1
COKE

2
PEPSI COLA

3
CROSSE & BLACKWELL

4
AQUA PURA DEER PARK

5
COKE

6
HAWAIIAN PUNCH

7
MINERAL SPRING

1
ALFALAVAL

2
JELL-O

3
CLEAR BROOK SPRING WATER

4
INDUSTRIA DE REFRIGERANTES C-AXIAS

5
JWANA JUICE

6
WISDOM BEVERAGE

7
PERRIER

1

4

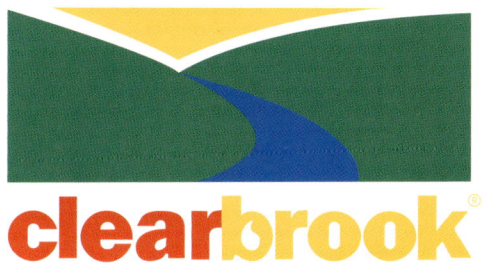

5

2

6

3

7

Winston Straight up

1

Interbrew

2

3

OB GATE

A GENUINE PLACE FOR GENUINE PEOPLE

4

5

6

BRITISH AMERICAN TOBACCO

7

1
WINSTON

2
INTERBREW

3
H.C.BERGER BREWING COMPANY

4
ORIENTAL BREWERY COMPANY "OB GATE"

5
DOMAINE HALEAUX

6
MILLER BREWING COMPANY

7
BRITISH AMERICAN TOBACCO

1
AUSTRAIAN BREWING CORPORATION

2
CHEAPSMOKES

3
ANGELIC BREWING COMPANY

4
BALD BEAVER BREWING COMPANY

5
JOHNNIE WALKER

6
THE MILLER BAND

7
SANTA BARBARA WINE AUCTION

1

4

JOHNNIE WALKER ®

5

CHEAPSMOKES

2

6

ANGELIC
BREWING CO.

3

SANTA BARBARA WINE AUCTION

7

S E N E S C O

1

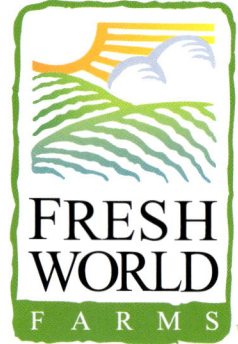

™

2

EXCEL.

smartchoice

• next generation •

3

AGRILIANCE

4

FRESH
WORLD
FARMS ™

5

Timberline

I N D U S T R I E S

6

P. Tavilla Co., Inc.

7

Alegria

W I N E R Y

8

1
SENESCO

2
LAND O'LAKES FARMLAND FEED

3
EXCEL

4
AGRILIANCE

5
DNA PLANT TECHNOLOGIES

6
TIMBERLINE INDUSTRIES

7
P.TAVILLA CO.,INC

8
ALEGRIA WINERY

1
PLEASANT RIDGE FARMS

2
HULINGSHOF

3
INCUBADDORA

4
GRIFFIN PRODUCTS

5
FOXTON FARM

6
BLOOMING HILLS FARM

7
ALPIA-AGRICULTURAL COOPERA-
TIVE

8
CHICKENVILLE

1

2

3

4

5

6

7

8

83

göt2b™
spa

1

CAMP ESPRIT

2

3

Caldera Spas

4

BEVERLY SUN TANNING

5

6

RIO CALIENTE
THF ALTERNATIVF SDA

7

1
GOT2B

2
ESPRIT CAMP

3
AQUA STAR

4
CALDERA SPAS

5
BEVERLY SUN TANNING

6
AQUATIC LEISURE INTERNATIONAL
Aquatic Leisure International

7
RIO CALIENTE THF ALTERNATIVF
SDA

1
SENECA LAKE WHALE WATCH

2
MATINEE ENTERTAINMENT

3
INLAND ENTERTAINMENT CORPOR-
ATION Inland

4
EISEBERGS SKATEPARK

5
SUMMIT COUNTY, COLORADO

6
MTM ENTERTAINMENT

7
TURNER ENTERTAINMENT

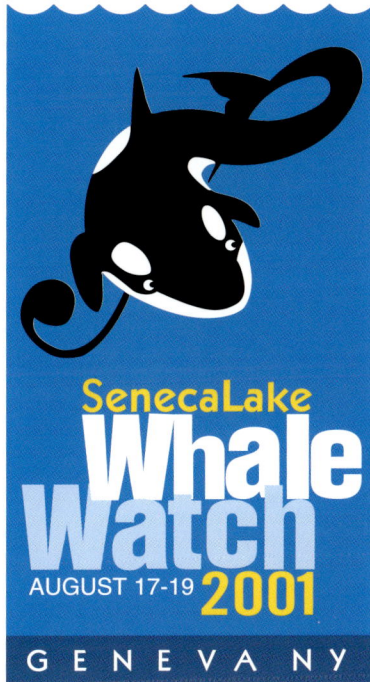

1

4

5

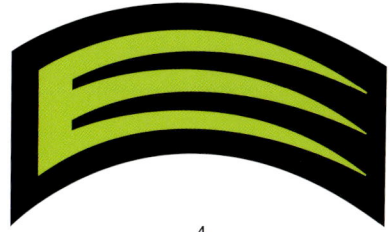

2

6

3

7

1

ALL-SUITE CASINO RESORT
LAS VEGAS

2

LAKEMARY
CENTER

3

GRAVITY
GAMES

4

Atrium
Le 1000
DE LA GAUCHETIERE

5

adelson entertainment

6

CENTRAL
QUEENS
YM & YWHA

7

McHAPPY DAY
MAY 6th, 1998

8

1
4 SEASONS FUN CLUB

2
ALL SUITE CASINO RESORT LAS
VEGAS

3
LAKEMARY CENTER

4
GRAITY GAMES

5
ATRIUM LE1000

6
ADELSON ENTERTAINMENT

7
CENTRAL QUEENS YM & YWHA

8
MCHAPPY DAY

1
NAPLES BATH TENNIS CLUB

2
DEER RUN COUNTRY CLUB

3
KONJIAM COUNTRY CLUB

4
THE AMELIA ISLAND CLUB

5
ROMORA BAY CLUB

6
FLAGSTAPP RANCH GOLF CLUB

7
MONTEREY BAY ATHLETIC CLUB

8
OCOTILLO ROCKET CLUB

Naples Bath Tennis Club
1

5

Deer Run Country Club
2

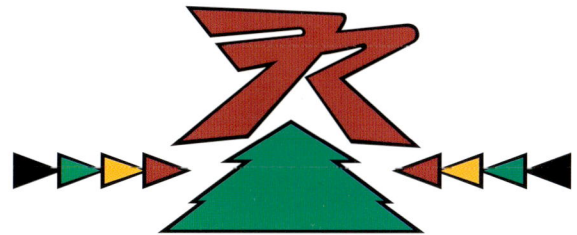
6

3

Monterey Bay Athletic Club
7

THE AMELIA ISLAND CLUB
4

Ocotillo TEST RANGE
8

Skaneateles Country Club

1

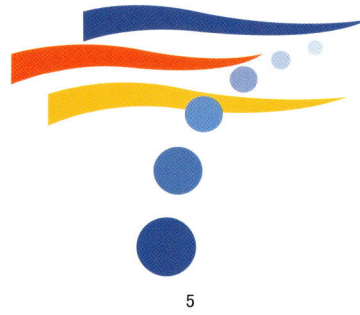

SEOWON VALLEY

Golf Club

2

COLOVISTA

COUNTRY CLUB

3

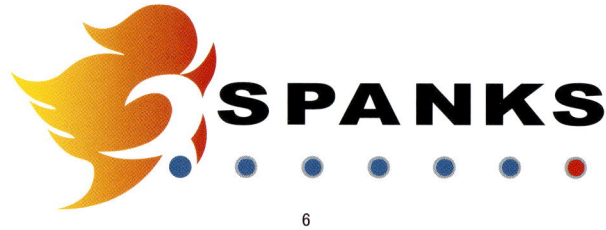

CHINJU COUNTRY CLUB

4

5

SPANKS

6

7

THE

WOOJUNG HILLS

COUNTRY CLUB

8

1
SKANEATELES COUNTRY CLUB

2
COLOVISTA COUNTRY CLUB

3
SPORTSWAVE COUNTRY CLUB

4
CHINJU COUNTRY CLUB

5
TAIKOYAMA COUNTY CLUB

6
SPANKS

7
CYCLE HEDZ

8
WOOJUNG HILLS COUNTRY CLUB

1
PARADISE GOLF

2
URESHINO ONSEN HIGHLAND GOLF
CLUB

3
DEL MAR THOROUGHBRED CLUB

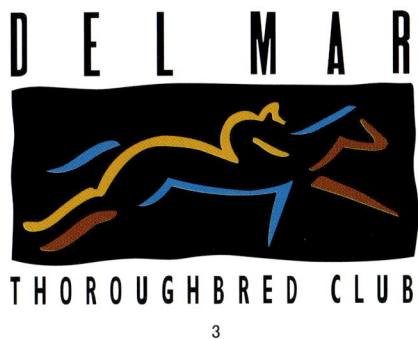

4
SHEPHERD GOLF

5
SANTA ANA GOLF CLUB

6
MS SOCIETY NYC CHAPTER

7
KO OLINA GOLF CLUB

Paradise Golf
1

shepherd
G O L F
4

5

**URESHINO
ONSEN
HIGHLAND
GOLF
CLUB**
2

THE
Manhattan
SOCIETY
6

D E L M A R
THOROUGHBRED CLUB
3

Ko Olina
7

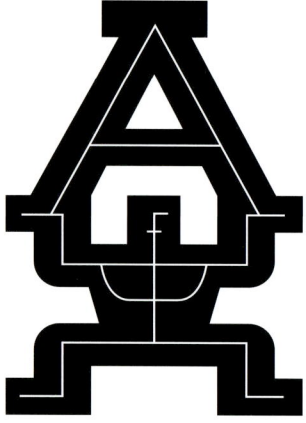

1

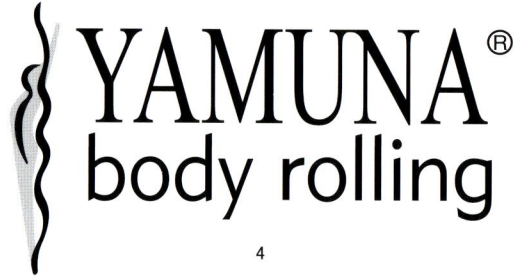

2

3

4

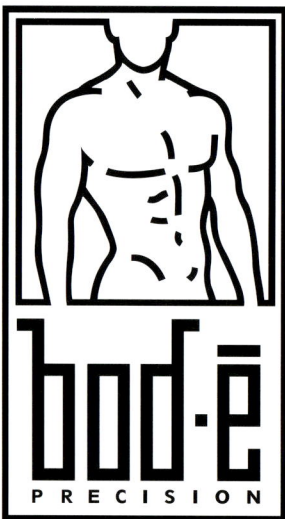

5

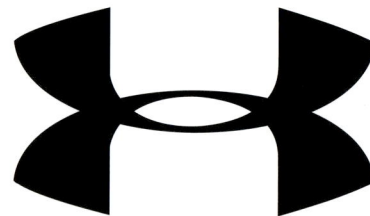

6

1
AUSTIN GYM

2
BEACON HILL CLUB

3
BOD-E

4
YAMUNA BODY ROLLING

5
ROUNDS

6
UNDER ARMOUR PERFORMANCE APPAREL

1
NSCE GENTRE

2
YOGAFIT TRAINING SYSTEMS

3
TANITA

4
GIANT STEPS

5
THE LITTLE GYM

6
HYDE PARK GYM

7
DK AROMATHERAPY

NSCE
Centre

1

giant steps

4

YogaFit®
Training Systems

2

THE Little
gym ®

5

6

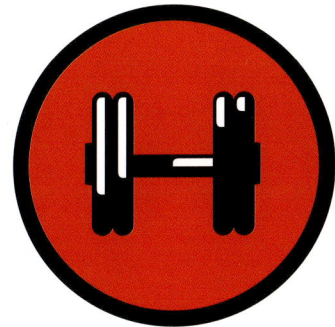

TANITA®
A Step Toward A Healthier Life.

3

DK Aromatherapy

7

91

1

2

3

4

5

6

1
LADIES' PACE FITNESS, INC

2
PURE YOGA

3
FITA FITNESS CENTER

4
HAPPY HEALTHY HABITS

5
ON-THE-GO FITNESS PRO

6
PHYSIQUE ENHANCEMENT

1
YOGA DEL MAR

2
PRANA

3
SANSARLA

4
BE YOGA

5
YOGA INTERNATIONAL

6
KRIPALU CENTER FOR YOGA &
HEALTH

7

1

2

3

4

5

6

7

1

5

1
JAVA DEPOT

2
PETERS

3
DUNIA CLUB

4
PENN STATE JAZZ CLUB

5
OMNI CLUB

6
VAPOR

7
LA CASA

2

4

6

3

7

1
BARNES WEST COUNTY HOSPITAL
COSMETIC SURGERY CENTER

2
AVENUE SKIN CARE

3
RESULTS FOR WOMEN

4
MELLEE SKIN CARE

5
ISIS

6
SHAVE EDGE

7
CLEOPATRA BEAUTY SALON & DAY
SPA

8
RELEASE HAIR PRODUCTS

1

5

2

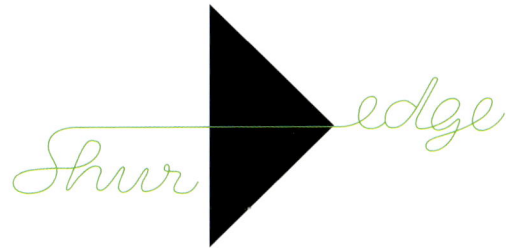

Results
for women™

3

Shur edge

6

CLEOPATRA
BEAUTY SALON & DAY SPA

7

Mellee Skin Care

4

RELEASE

8

1

2

3

4

5

6

7

1
NIVEA PATRNERING WITH YOU
TO BRING OUT THE BEST IN
YOUR SKIN

2
MOEN

3
VEET

4
SOSMOOTH FOR HEALTHY HAIR
WITH A SMOOTH ATTITUDE

5
REVERSION COSMETICS

6
AU-STAR

7
ELIZABETH ARDEN

1
BLISTEX

2
SLAVE

3
CABOODLES

4
DIOSSI COSMETICS

5
ANASTASIA MARIE COSMETICS
Anastasia Marie Cosmetics

6
H₂O

7
PLACE LAURIER

Blistex Lip Tone

1

diossi cosmetics

4

SLAVE

2

5

H 2

6

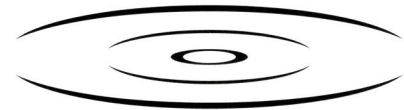

caboodles®

3

PlaceLaurier

7

A V O N

the company for women

1

~H2O+™

WATER IS YOU.™

5

face today
with new confidence

2

6

Face
TODAY
with new confidence

3

7

face today
with new & confidence

4

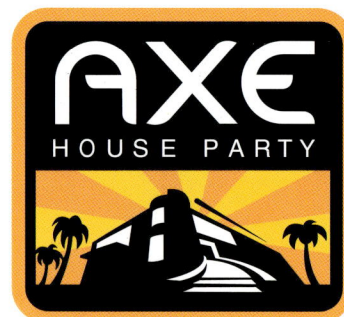

8

BROCATO

1

2

3

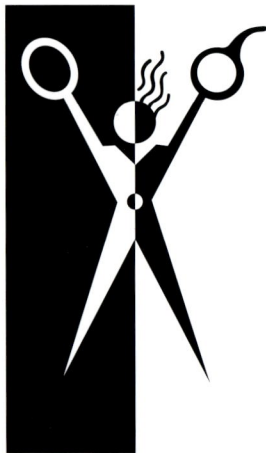

4

5

HAIR PEACE

6

7

SYLVESTRE
FRANC
SALON

8

1
VERDE COMMUNICATIONS

2
PURPLE MOON

3
PLANET SALON

4
JAMES ALAN SALON

5
EAST 3

6
HAIR PEACE HAIR SALON

7
AMBER LEAR

8
SYLVESTRE FRANC/HAIR SALON

1
IMAGE HAIRSTYLING

2
MARK BERGSMA

3
HAIR SALON

4
REBECCA CUTTER—HAIR STYLIST

5
SHEARS

6
JUST KIDS HAIR SALON

7
LA MOP HAIR STUDIO

8
SUNSHINE HAIR DESIGN & DAY SPA

1

6

2

4

7

3

5

8

DARK HORSE CLOTHING

1

montrail ™

4

L'ORÉAL
PARiS

5

V

2

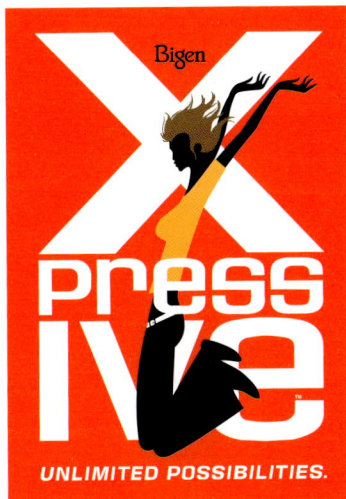

ALLIGATOR

6

press
ive

UNLIMITED POSSIBILITIES.

3

7

1

5

CRANE

2

BabyTalk
MATERNITY PROGRAM
STORE

3

6

NiQ NaQ

4

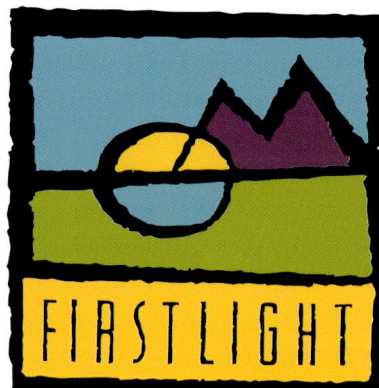

FIRSTLIGHT

7

1
SOLO EDITIONS

2
MIRAGE

3
COLUMBIA SPORTSWEAR COMPANY

4
LONDON FOG

5
JORDACHE

6
NORS SPORT

7
FOX

8
SCOTLAND YARDS

1

JEANS • TOPS • BELTS

5

2

6

3

7

4

8

1

2

3

5

23

6

4

7

1
СПОРТИВНЫЕ СУПЕРМАРКЕТЫ
СПОРТМАСТЕР

2
OSHKOSH

3
THE LRG CLOTHING COMPANY

4
STIETCH CAPRI LEE

5
SWELL FASHION

6
"23"

7
GIG WEAR SOHO NEW YORK

1
TINBERLAND

2
L'ATTESA

3
URBAN OUTFITTERS FASHION STORE

4
AQILAS

5
JM EMBROIDERY

6
PROPPER AMERICAN

7
HAPPY CHIX SHOP

1

J M EMBROIDERY

5

2

URBAN

3

6

4

7

1

3

KIDS

The Original
bobux®

4

Buster Brown & Co.

2

greendog™

5

1
IT'S COCONUT

2
BUSTER BROWN & CO.
The Kids Division Of Broon

3
KOO KOO BEAR KIDS

4
BOBUX

5
GREEN DOG

1
EURO ROSE KNITWEAR LIMITED

2
WARDROBE

3
ELEGANT CREATIONS

4
HANNAH FLAMING

5
CHIVANT

6
RED FOX

7
PAINT JOCKEYS

1

4

2

5

6

3

7

1

BROWN SHOE

5

THE
TERRITORY
AHEAD

2

6

3

Foot Locker®

4

7

1
BLUE SPHERE

2
MAMMY VILLAGE

3
BUSKINS BABY SHOES

4
AMERICAN GIRL TODAY

5
FINISH LINE

6
ECKO RED

7
CORPORATE INNOVATIONS

8
TOPIX

5

1

6

2

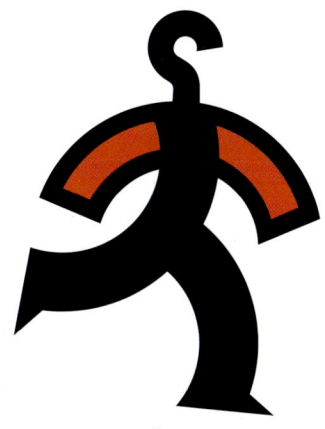

7

3

4

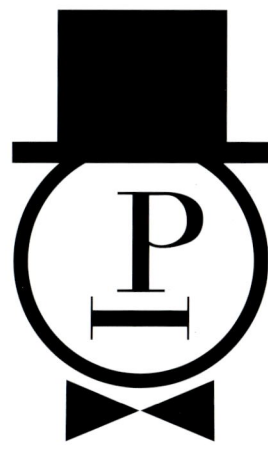

8

1

2

5

3

6

4

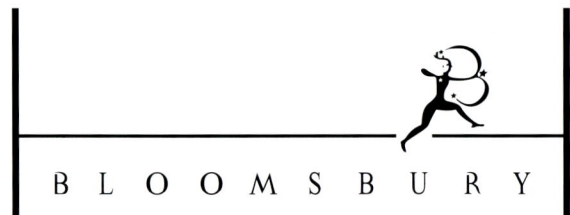

7

1
RICHARD LYNN'S SHOE MARKET

2
BOYER SPORTS

3
FISH OUT OF WATER

4
ECNORROT MENSWEAR

5
SLOWBURN CLOTHING CO

6
EXPLORE

3

1

4

2

5

6

Inglesina®

1

2

6

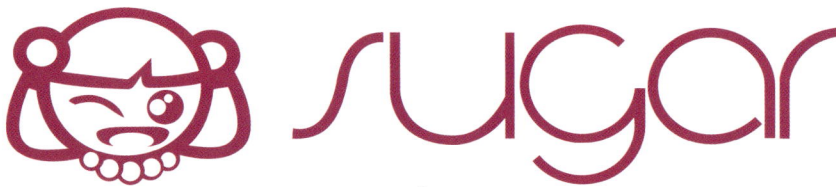

3

4

7

POLARTEC®

5

1
HO

2
TUFF HEART

3
SWATCH SKIN

4
PATEK PHILIPPE

5
ROLEX

6
BREGUETD

7
CLIC TIME

1

TUFFHEART

2

swatch® SKIN

3

PATEK PHILIPPE
GENEVE

4

ROLEX

5

Breguet
Depuis 1775

6

clic TIME

7

HEARTS ON FIRE®

1

KEYSTONE®

2

LOO creations

3

SITARA Networks™

4

daniele trissi

5

HODSON JEWELRY GALLERIES

6

Doris Panos

7

V

8

TABU™

9

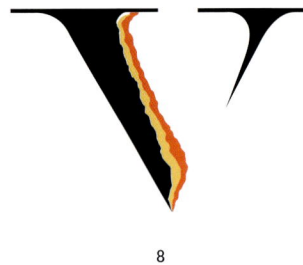

1
ANAHEIM RESORT

2
ADIRONDACKS

3
CANADA

4
GUTSY WOMEN TRAVEL

5
IRELAND

6
CHARLESTON COUNTY PARK & RE-
CREATION COMMISSION

7
OWN HARBOUR TOWN HILTON HEA-
D ISLAND

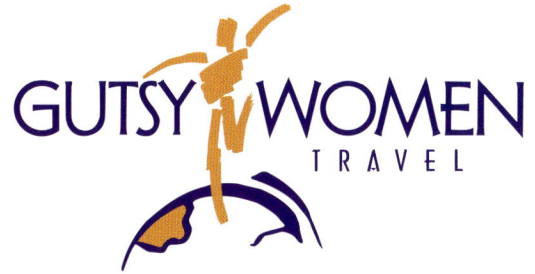

4

1

5

2

6

3

7

117

HoliMont

1

MIAMI

2

5

3

6

seattle

4

LA CASA DEL ZORRO
DESTRE RESORT

7

1
THOMSON SAFARIS A DIVISION OF
WINELAND–THOMSON ADVENTTURES,
INC

2
POLSKA

3
SOUTH CAROLINA

4
LOS.CABOS

5
BUSINESS TRAVEL NW

6
JULIAN TOUR

7
MALAYSIA

1

4

5

2

6

3

7

1

4

1
PAPAYA BEACH

2
ST.PETERSBURG

3
WELCOME

4
SAN DIEGO

5
MISSISSIPPI

6
TURKEY

7
ALBUQUERQUE CONVENTION & VISITORS BUREAU

Mississippi. We can do that.

5

2

6

3

7

1
EAGLE CAP EXCURSION TRAIN

2
IMOYA SOUTH AFRICAN TOUR G-
ROUPS

3
TUCSON

4
PORTUGAL

5
ESPANA

6
TURKEY

7
HELLENIC TOURIST PROPERTIES

8
HAWAII'S BIG ISLAND

1

5

2

6

3

7

4

8

121

Drayton Hall

1

2

Fort Smith
ARKANSAS

3

Hawaii's Big Island

4

TROPICOOL
MIAMI
GREATER MIAMI AND THE BEACHES

5

А.ЧУБАЙС

EX LIBRIS

6

BALD HEAD ISLAND

7

1
DRAYTON HALL

2
SAMHONG TRAVEL AGENCY

3
FORT SMITH ARKANSAS

4
HAWAII'S BIG ISLAND

5
TROPICOOL MIAMI GREATER MIA-
MI AND THE BEACHES

6
A.TCHUBAIS

7
BALD HEAD ISLAND

1
CARIBBEAN TOURISM ORGANIZAT-
ION

2
BLUE DEEP

3
KISSIMMEE ST.CLOUD FLORIDA

4
MONTANA

5
AEGEAN TOURS LLP

6
NEW ORLEANS

7
ITALIA

8
GEORGIA

1

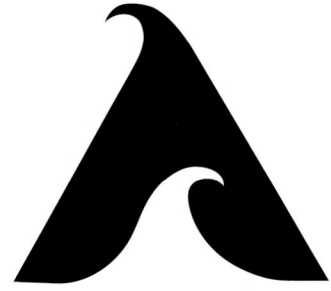
5

2

6

7

3

4

8

123

Zazublu™

1

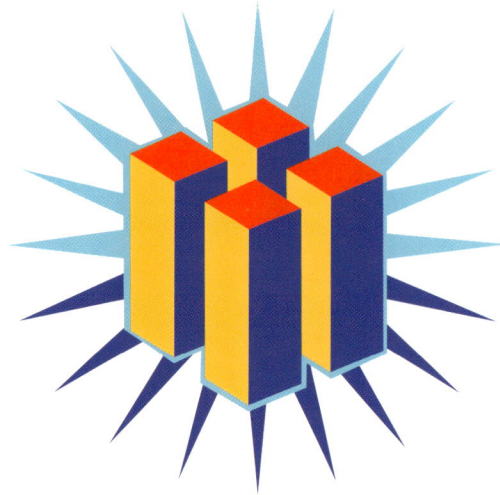

VOYAGER TRAVEL

2

Holland™

3

MetroViews, Inc.

4

1
ZAZUBLU COMPANY

2
VOYAGER TRAVEL

3
HOLLAND

4
METROVIEWS.INC

5
AROUND TOWN CITY-WIDE ENTER-
TAINMENT DIRECTORY

6
KARITEE

7
LATIN CRUISES & EXPEDITIONS

5

Karitee

6

LATIN
Cruises & Expeditions

7

1
HAHN FORISTAL TRAVEL MANAGE-
MENT.INC.

2
SEATTLE CONVENTION & VISITO-
RS BUREAU

3
AUSTRIALIA

4
NEW MEXICO

5
THE RIVER WALK SAN ANTONIO

6
NEGOMBO

7
MALTA

HAHN·FORISTAL
Travel Management, Inc.
1

4

THE RIVER WALK SAN ANTONIO
5

2

NEGOMBO
6

3

MALTA
7

125

bc's
family fishing
weekend

1

CAYMAN
ISLANDS

2

H.
Harrison

3

mountain creek™

4

5

LONG ISLAND ™

6

CROSS
COUNTRY
TravCorps

7

1
BC'S FAMILY FISHING WEEKEND

2
CAYMAN ISLANDS

3
HARRISON

4
MOUNTAIN CREEK

5
POINTS TRAVEL

6
LONG ISLAND

7
CROSS COUNTRY TRAVCORPS

1
KANGBUGU

2
TARGET GREATLAND OUTDOORS

3
GUAM

4
RANGER

5
APPLIED TRAVEL INTELLIGENCE

6
MERIDIAN HOLIDAYS

7
THE LEISURE COMPANY

1

4

Applied Travel Intelligence
5

2

MERIDIAN HOLIDAYS
6

GUAM
3

The Leisure Company
7

1

2

5

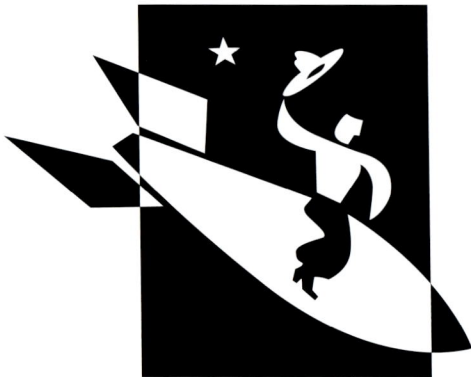

3

TUMI

HAVE A SAFE TRIP.

6

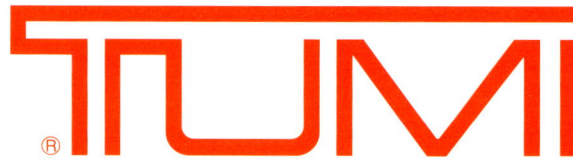

4

7

1
MARIANAS VISTORS AUTHORITY

2
MISSOURI

3
PEGASUS TRAVEL

4
OUTRIGGER WAIKOLOA BEACH

5
WHITE CYPRES LAKES

6
SKI LAKE TAHOE

7
PRIMAVERA LABORATORIES.INC

1

4

5

2

6

3

7

Paradise
Safari Park Hotel
— Nairobi —

1
THE LODGE TORREY PINES

2
DAYS INN

3
ALIDI/STANDARD HOTEL

4
ALMA VIVERE IN TUTTI I SENSI

5
EXECUTIVE RESIDENCES

6
BEST WESTERN

7
DOUBLE TREE

1

alma
vivere in tutti i sensi

4

EXECUTIVE RESIDENCES
Marriott

5

DAYS INN

2

Best Western

6

3

DOUBLE TREE

7

131

SkyDome Hotel
1

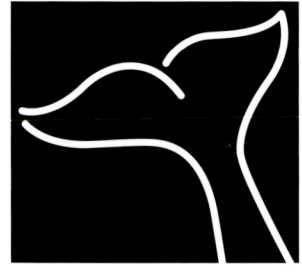

marc suites
5

2

6

Hotel Santa Fe
3

4

7

1
HER THAI RESTAURANT

2
RESTOS PLAISIRS

3
BATAVIA NURSING&CONVALESCENT
INN

4
LA QUINTA INN

5
GRAND HOTEL

6
HOTEL FLORA

7
EAGLERIDGE

4

1

5

2

6

3

7

133

FOUR SEASONS
Hoteli and Reiorti

1

2

3

SIX CONTINENTS

4

5

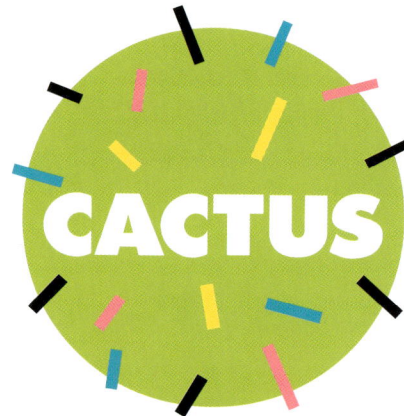

6

HACIENDA
DEL MAR

7

1
FOUR SEASONS

2
TROPICAL JUNGLE

3
CIBO

4
SIX CONTINENTS

5
PARIS LAS VEGAS

6
CACTUS

7
HACIENDA DELMAR

1
ZUIHO HOTEL

2
NORTHSTAR AT TAHOE

3
SOCIETE DES BAINS DE MER MO–
NTE CARLO

4
SPRING HILL SUITES

5
HILTON

6
PICANTE RESTAURANT

7
HYATT INTERNATIONAL GRAND H–

8
HILTON INTERNATIONAL GUAM

HOTEL
ZUIHO
1

Hilton
5

northstar
at tahoe.
2

Picante
6

SOCIÉTÉ DES BAINS DE MER
MONTE CARLO
3

NELAYAN
7

SpringHill
SUITES
4

Hilton International
Guam
8

135

1

2

THE HOTEL JULIANA

3

MORAY'S

4

5

6

AFFINIA DUMONT

7

PARADISE

8

1
GRAND WAILEA RESORT

2
GREEN VALLEY SPA ST GEORGE U-
TAH

3
LITTLE ST.SIMONS ISLAND

4
SANDESTIN

5
SHUTTERS

6
VACATION RESORTS INTERNATIO-
NAL

7
CHARMING INNS INC

Sandestin
4

Grand Wailea Resort
HOTEL & SPA
Maui
1

Shutters®
5

GREEN VALLEY SPA
ST. GEORGE, UTAH
2

VACATION RESORTS
INTERNATIONAL
6

LITTLE
ST. SIMONS
ISLAND
3

Charming Inns®
I N C .
7

1

2

3

4

5

6

7

1
LAPLAND LAKE

2
WATER.COLOR INN

3
ROCK RESORTS

4
OSPREY

5
NEW COUPLE

6
LAKE AUSTIN SPA RESORT

7
THE BREAKERS

138

RANCHO LA PUERTA

1

LAPLAYA

BEACH & GOLF RESORT

4

THE ISLAND CLUB

Great Exuma • Bahamas

2

5

Ski Butternut

6

Neville
Log Homes

3

THE
BERKSHIRES

7

EAST·WEST RESORTS

1

Golf Lodging™

2

S T A R W O O D

3

4

WILLOWS

5

MAUNA LANI RESORT

6

CAREFREE RESORT & VILLAS

7

1
EMERALD BAY GREAT EXUMA BAHAMAS

2
TURTLE CAY BEACH RESORT

3
THE ASIAN SPA

4
CONNECTICUT RIVER VALLEY SHORELINE

5
WATERSIDE

6
GRAND ISLE

7
POINTE SOUTH MOUNTAIN RESORT

4

1

5

2

6

3

7

1

2

3

1
CHILDREN'S ZOO

2
HEALESVILLE SANCTUARY

3
BROOKFIELD ZOO

4
COLUMBIAN PARK ZOO

5
CARLTON PLANTS

6
AMELIA ISLAND PLANTATION

7
BUTTERFLY WING SAINT LOUIS ZOO

8
HIPPO BEACH

CHILDREN'S ZOO

1

2

3

Columbian Park ZOO
Lafayette Parks & Recreation

4

CARLTON
PLANTS

5

Amelia Island Plantation®

6

BUTTERFLY WING
SAINT LOUIS ZOO

7

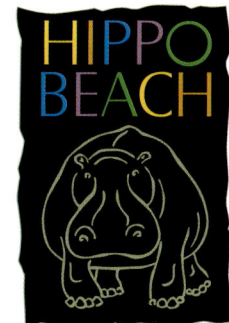

HIPPO BEACH

8

1

ROCKY COASTS

SENECA PARK ZOO

5

ZOO FARI

FEAST with the BEASTS

2

6

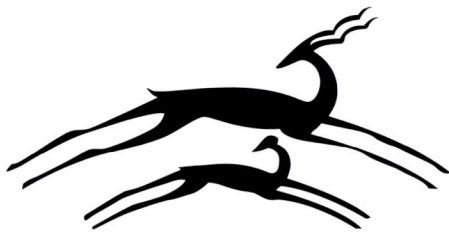

DALLAS ZOO

3

+KOTA

7

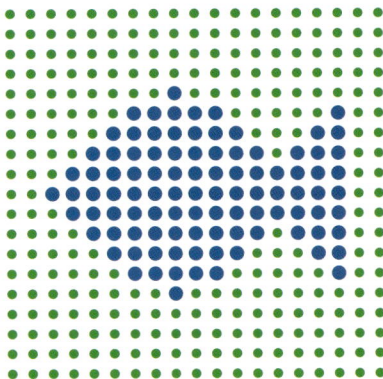

4

8

1
LOS MARINEROS Los

2
THE PHOENIX ZOO

3
DALLAS ZOO

4
OKINAWA AQUARIUM

5
ROCKY COASTS SENECA PARK ZOO

6
PITTSBURGH ZOO

7
+KOTA

8
B-WILD

1
KATONAH MUSEUM OF ART

2
RED MOUNTAIN PARK

3
ARKANSAS STATE PARKS

4
CHESAPEAKE CHILDREN MUSEUM

5
FRIENDS OF LSLAMORADA AREA
ATATE PARKS

6
SEASEA MULTI—HULLS

7
LAKE POWELL

8
LEWIS & CLARK A NORTH DAKOTA

1

5

RED MOUNTAIN PARK
2

6

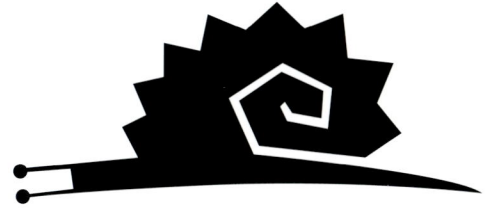
Arkansas State Parks
3

Lake Powell™
7

CHESAPEAKE Children's MUSEUM
4

LEWIS & CLARK™
A North Dakota Adventure
8

145

Riverfront Park™

1

TURTLE BAY
EXPLORATION PARK

2

Wesley Village

3

4

DISCOVERY COVE®
ORLANDO

5

TULSA PARKS

6

MONTEREY BAY
AQUARIUM

7

1
RIVERFRONT PARK

2
TURTLE BAY

3
WESLEY VILLAGE

4
PUBLIC PARK IN PITTSBUEGH

5
DISCOVERY COVE ORLANDO

6
TULSA PARKS

7
MONTEREY BAY AQUARIUM

1
MUSEUM VICTORIA

2
AMERICAN MUSEUM OF NATURAL H-
ISTORY

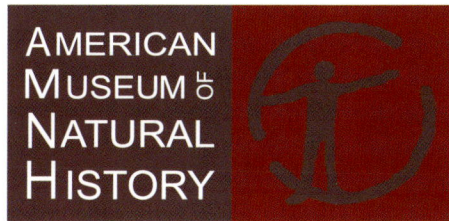

3
J.PAUL GETTY MUSEUM

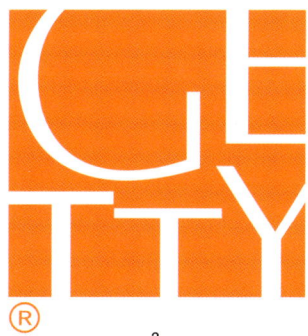

4
VANDERBILT MUSEUM

5
AFRICAN—AMERICAN MUSEUM

6
SCIENCEWORKS MUSEUM

7
ANNETTE GREEN MUSEUM AT THE
FRAGRANCE FOUNDATION MUSEUM

147

1

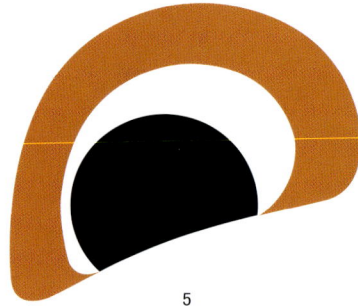

2

3

4

5

6

7

1
BERSTROM

2
THE ALBUQUERQUE MUSEUM

3
NEW MEXICO MUSEUM

4
CHILDREN MUSEUM OF MAINE

5
EDO TOKYO MUSEUM

6
YOKOHAMA CHARACTER MUSEUM

7
HOUSTON CHILDREN MUSEUM

1
NATIONAL MUSEUM OF SCIENCE

2
TEPCO

3
SOUTHWEST MUSEUM

4
MUSEUM VICTORIA

5
MADAME TUSSAUD

6
THE MUSEUM OF SCIENCE AND IN-
DUSTRY

7
THE MIGHTY EIGHTH AIR FORCE
HERITAGE MUSEUM

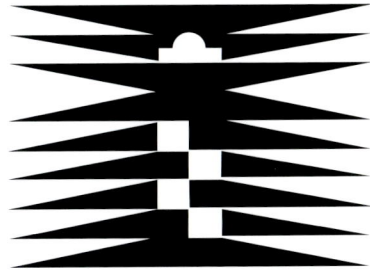

1

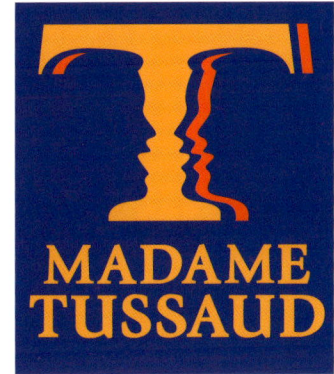

5

2

3

6

4

7

1

KidsVision

2

NOVA MEDICS

3

Touch CHIROPRACTIC

4

5

6

SPINE AND SPORTS MEDICINE

7

1
HARVARD MEDICAL SCHOOL

2
KIDS VISION

3
NOVA MEDICS
Nova Medics

4
TOUCH CHIROPRACTIC

5
THE CHILDREN'S HOSPITAL

6
PRATT REGIONAL MEDICAL

7
SPINE AND SPORTS MEDICINE

1
MONTE VISTA SMALL ANIMAL H-
OSPITAL

2
LENOX HILL HEART AND VASC-
ULAR INSTITUTE OF NEW
YORK

3
CHILD GUIDANCE CLINIC

4
WESTLAKE SURGCAL CENTER

5
ST.JOHN'S HOSPITAL

6
HEART HOSPITAL OF NEW MEXCO

7
THE CREDIT VALLEY HOSPITAL

8
HOSPITAL FOR SPECIAL SURGERY

Monte Vista
small animal hospital

1

5

**Lenox Hill
Heart and Vascular
Institute
of New York**

2

6

3

C R E D I T · V A L L E Y
THE CREDIT VALLEY HOSPITAL

7

**WESTLAKE
SURGICAL**
C E N T E R

4

8

CHRISTINA FIELDS
CIBTAC. A.o.R. Pract. Assoc. MAR.
Clinical Reflexolgist
1

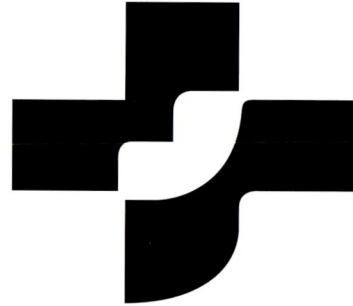

2

HOOPP
3

5

West Shore Christian Hospital
6

7

4

PIONEER
HOSPITALS
8

1
CHRISTINA FIELDS

2
AZZOLINO CHIROPRACTIC NEURO-
LOGY GROUP

3
HOSPITALS OF ONTARIO PENSION
PLAN

4
WASHINGTON HAND SURGERY CEN-
TER

5
UISAN HOSPITAL

6
WEST SHORE CHRISTIAN HOSPITAL

7
GASTROENTEROLOGY SPECIALISTS
OF LEXINGTON
Lexington

8
PIONEER HOSPITALS

1
PRACTICAL PET CARE

2
AMERICAN DIABETES ASSOCIATION

3
H.E.E.D

4
AMERICAN LUNG ASSOCIATION

5
ALEXANDRA DOCTOR'S NETWORK

6
DELAWARE CANCER NETWORK

7
AMERICAN ASSOCIATION OF SPI-
NAL CORD INJURY NURSES

Practical Pet Care
Your essential online pet care resource

1

AMERICAN LUNG ASSOCIATION®

4

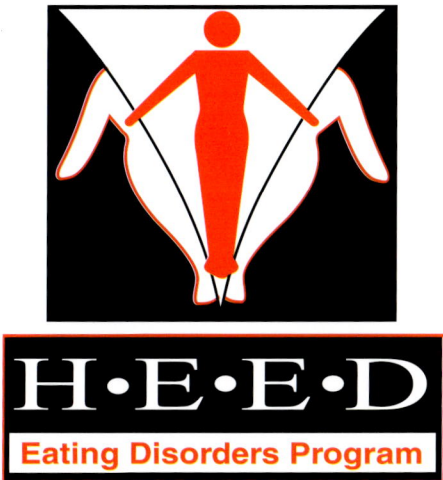

2

5

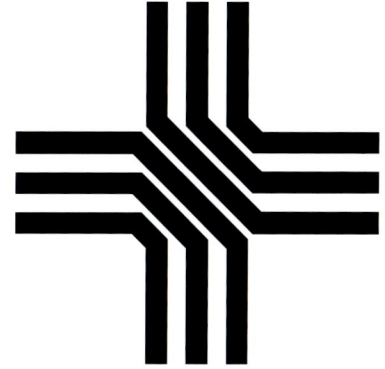

DELAWARE CANCER NETWORK

6

H•E•E•D
Eating Disorders Program

3

7

153

1

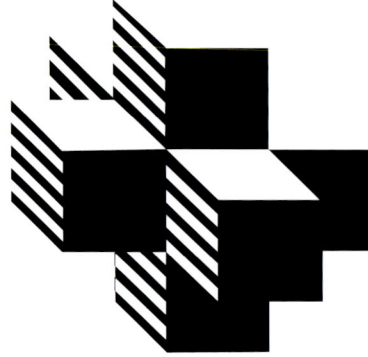

2

3

5

6

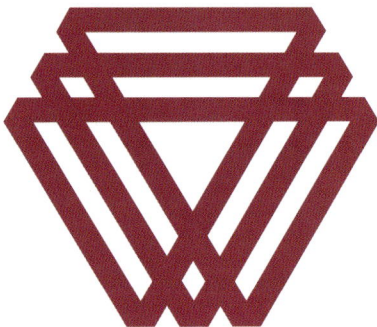

4

7

1
ZMED

2
ANIKA THERAPEUTICS

3
BAY AREA JEWISH HEALING CENTER

4
VIRGINIA LNTEGRATED PHYSICIANS

5
NATIONAL SURGERY CENTERS INC

6
MEDICAL HELP

7
CRYO.CARE

1
MERCK HEARTGUARD

2
MAITRI AIDS HOSPICE

3
PULSAR INTERNATIONAL

4
VASTECH

5
ACUENT

6
ZENECA PHARMACEUTICAL CO-
RP

7
PCS HEALTH SYSTEMS INC

8
CARDIO NET

1

5

2

6

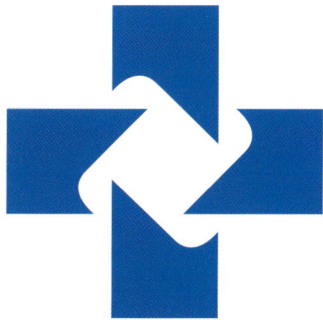

3

7

4

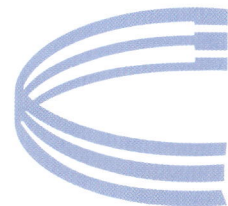

8

Advanced Medicine

1

2

The May Eye Care Center & Associates

3

Centro da Mãe

4

5

Inland Northwest
Cancer Centers

The hope to cure. The Promise to care.

6

7

THE BLOOD CENTER

8

1
ADVANCED MEDICINE

2
LANE MAMMOGRAPHY CENTER WOM-
AN'S HEALTHCARE

3
MECCA(THE MAY EYE CARE CEN-
TER & ASSOCIATES)

4
CENTRO DA MAE

5
OVARIAN CANCER DETECTION &
PREVENTION CENTER

6
INLAND NORTHWEST CANCER CEN-
TERS

7
CHIRO NET

8
THE BLOOD CENTER

156

1
WEST ASSOCIATES

2
PRIORITY PHYSIQUES

3
REMSCHEIDER GESPRACHE

4
SUSQUENANNA ADDICTIONS CEN-
TER

5
HORIZON HEALTH CARE GROUP

6
LIND BUTLER PSYCHOTHERAPY

7
LASER & SKIN AESTHETICS C-
ENTER

1

SUSQUENANNA ADDICTIONS CENTER

4

Priority Physiques

2

5

Lind Butler PSYCHOTHERAPY

6

Remscheider Gespräche

3

LASER & SKIN AESTHETICS CENTER

7

157

1

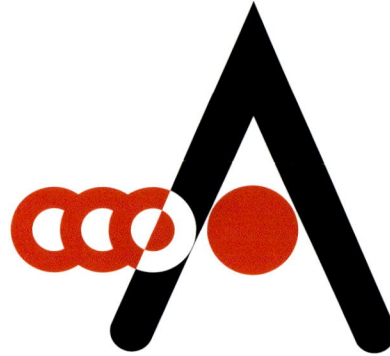

5

2

6

3

7

4

8

1
DEPARTMENT OF HEALTH & HU-
MAN SERVICES USA

2
CANCER RESEARCH INSTITUTE

3
HEALTHCARE STAFFING
Hpo

4
HUMAN GENOME SCIENCES

5
MEDCHEM

6
NUESOFT HEALTHCARE SOLUT-
IONS

7
HEALTH BANKE

8
BOTANICAL REMEDY RESEARCH
INC

1
TRUEVISION LASER CENTER

2
BABY BANKS

3
KEHRS MILL FAMILY DENTAL CA-
RE

4
QUEST DIAGNOSTICS INCORPORA-
TED

5
NORTH COAST

6
VITAL GREEN CO.LTD

7
NORTHEAST MEDICAL CENTER

8
AMERICAN MEDICAL CENTER

1

5

2

6

3

7

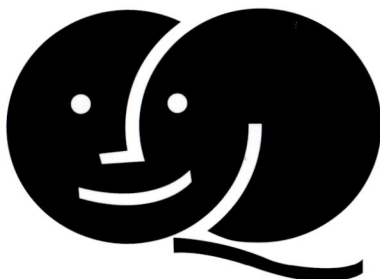

4

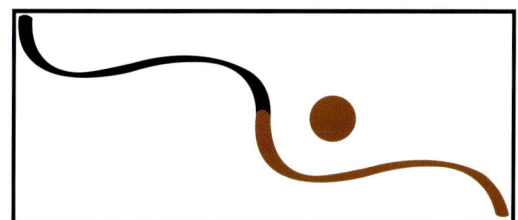

8

1

華埠健康診所
CHINATOWN HEALTH CLINIC

2

Van Romer Chiropractic

3

PilgrimsVeterinaryClinic

4

5

6

7

1
DR.ROSS MARCHETTA

2
CHINATOWN HEALTH CLINIC

3
VAN ROMER CHIROPRACTIC

4
PILGRIMS VETERINARY CLINIC

5
ON WO TONG

6
CLEVELAND CLINIC

7
UNIERSITY CHIROPRACTIC CLINIC

1
DR.DANGSTORP

2
PRESTONWOOD DENTAL

3
BOOKLINE DENTAL STUDIO

4
KAPUST DDS

5
SUSAN M LOVE MD

6
PRO ACTION

7
BELL DENTAL

1

4

2

5

PRO**ACTION**

6

3

BELL DENTAL

7

161

1

ADVANCED
SPINE & REHAB, P.C.
at Val vista Lakes

2

3

MᶜLEAN COUNTY
PRENATAL CLINIC

4

5

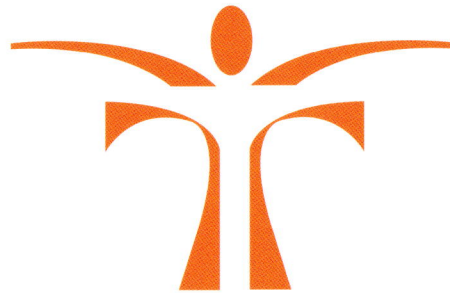

THERAPEUTIC
T O U C H

6

Brookside Ob/Gyn

7

1
DR.GEORG LEITL

2
ADVANCED SPINE & REHAB.P.C

3
MCLEAN COUNTY PREGNANCY CLIN-
IC

4
MCLEAN COUNTY PRENATAL CLINIC

5
PACIFIC OAKS

6
THERAPEUTIC TOUCH

7
BROOKSIDE OB/GYN

1
VALLEY COMMUNITY CLINIC

2
HOWARD'S OPTIQUE

3
ARC CLINIC

4
THE PEDERSON-KRAG MENTAL HE-
ALTH CENTER

5
SKIN'N'BONES

6
SUNSET BLVD

7
SIGNATURE

Valley
Community
Clinic

1

The Pederson–Krag
Center

4

2

5

Athlete
Reconditioning
Clinic

3

6

SIGNATURE

PLASTIC SURGERY

7

163

1

5

1
DONG A PHARMACEUTICAL

2
UNIMED

3
BAYER

4
BRIDGE MEDICAL

5
MILLENIUM PHARMACEUTICALS

6
MIYAGAWA PHARMACY

UNIMED

2

Bayer

BAYER

3

6

B R I D G E

4

1
THE MEDICINES COMPANY

2
CENTOCOR

3
WHOLE HEALTH PHARMACY INC

4
MERCK

5
BASELITE CORP.

6
ATLAS MEDICAL INTERNATIONAL

7
LONGER LIFE EXPECTANCY

1

5

2

3

6

4

7

1

2

3

4

5

6

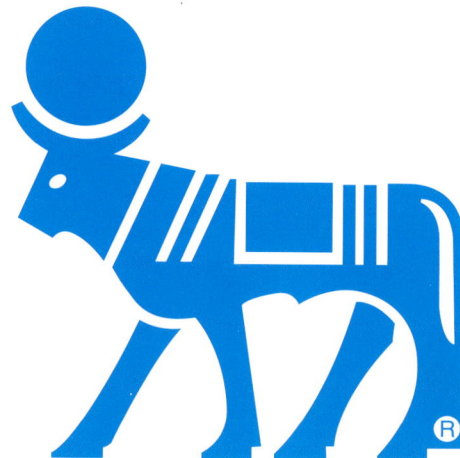

7

1
ERGOTRON

2
ABBOTT LAB

3
SPITZNER ARZNEIMITTEL

4
XENICAL

5
NEXIUM

6
AVENTIS

7
NOVO NORDISK

1
ATHENS MEDICAL GROUP

2
DAVID PHARMACEUTICALS.INC

3
NOVARTIS

4
PREMPRO

5
SCHERING-PLOUGH

6
PREMPRO

7
ABBOTT LAB

1

4

5

2

6

7

3

1

2

3

4

5

6

7

1
MONUROL

2
REMINYL

3
PROZAC

4
CELEXA CITALOPRAM HBR

5
STREPSILS PLUS

6
HEIGHT MAX SUPPLEMENTS FOR
YONG ADULTS

7
ACTONEL

1
RAINBOW

2
THERA SEED FOR PROSTATE CA-
NCER

3
EXELON

4
DETROL LA

5
EVOXAC

6
GLUCOTROL XL

3

1

4

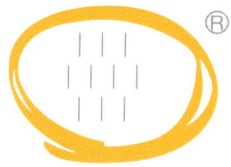

For Prostate Cancer

2

5

6

1

2

3

5

Maternal
Concepts
6

Franciscan Health Community
4

SUNFLOWER
HOLISTIC
Home Health Care, LLC
7

1
US BABY

2

3
NW NATURAL

4
FRANCISCAN HEALTH COMMUNI-
TY

5

6
MATERNAL CONCEPTS

7
SUNFLOWER HOLISTIC

1
NAVY FITNESS

2
MIST SPA

3
PROJECT FIT AMERICA

4
ACTIVE HEALTH.LNC.

5
MAXI-COSI

6
VITAMITE HEALTH PRODUCTS

7
GLOBAL HEALTH ALLIANCE

8
KYNETICS

NAVY FITNESS
1

AH!
4

MAXI·COSI®
5

THE Mist spa
2

Vitamite
Health Products
6

GLOBAL HEALTH ALLIANCE
7

PROJECT FIT AMERICA
3

kynetics
8

1

MUTUAL FUND
OneSource ™

2

3

SAGE
WEALTH PRESERVATION

4

1
PIN.POINT

2
ONE SOURCE MUTUAL FUND

3
VMF CAPITAL

4
SAGE WEALTH PRESERVATION

5
THE BALANCED OPPORTUNITY FUND

6
PATRIOT FINANCIAL USA

7
GLOBAL INVESTMENT SYSTEMS

THE BALANCED
OPPORTUNITY FUND

5

PATRIOT
FINANCIAL USA

6

Global
Investment
Systems

7

1
AIM

2
BERGER FUNDS

3
GEOTRUST

4
RHONE-POULENC

5
DERIVIUM CAPITAL

6
IVERSON

7
TALARIAN

8
ANNUITY BUYERS USA

AIM

1

DERIVIUM CAPITAL

5

BERGER FUNDS

2

Iverson

6

GeoTrust SM

3

Talarian

7

RHÔNE-POULENC

4

ANNUITY BUYERS USA

8

PACIFIC
Empire Lending, Inc.

1

LOWRY HILL

2

ARGO
Data Resource Corporation

3

ALLMERICA
FINANCIAL℠

4

5

Taihei

6

Bolsa de Valencia

7

1
PACIFIC EMPIRE LENDING INC

2
LOWRY HILL

3
ARGO DATA RESOURCE CORPORA-
TION

4
ALLMERICA FINANCIAL

5
KANSAS CITY CHAMBER OF COM-
MERCE

6
TAIHEI

7
BOLSA DE VALENCIA

1
VECTOR

2
HALABY INTERNATIONAL

3
DELOITTE TOUCHE TECHNOLOGY
FAST 500

4
PARAGON CAPITAL

5
STUDENT LOAN

6
DEUTSCHE BORSE

7
EXECUTIVE LENDING GROUP

8
TROIKA DIALOG

1

eStudent Loan

5

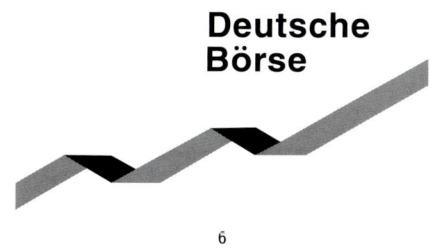

2

Deutsche Börse

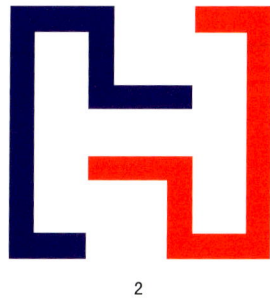

6

Executive Lending
GROUP

7

DELOITTE & TOUCHE
TECHNOLOGY
FAST 500

3

PARAGON
CAPITAL

4

TROIKA DIALOG

8

PROGRESSIVE
LENDING LLC

1

COMPANY
ANALYST

5

SP DR®

2

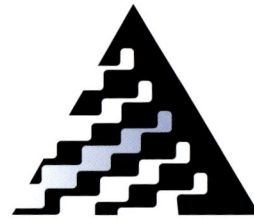

PERSUMMA
FINANCIAL SM

6

HSS
Funding
www.hssfunding.com

3

ifc

4

Begin today.

Mutual of Omaha

7

1
PROGRESSIVE LENDING LLC

2
SPDR

3
HSS FUNDING

4
IFC CENTRAL WATERFRONT PRO-
PERTY

5
COMPANY ANALYST

6
PERSUMMA FINANCIAL

7
MUTUAL OF OMAHA

1
ALEXANDRA CHAMBER OF COMMERCE

2
GREATER MINNEAPOLIS CHAMBER
OF COMMERCE

3
INDIGOPOOL.COM

4
RZB GROUP

5
GAB ROBINS

6
BARKERS

7
SAN JUAN BAUTISTA CHAMBER OF
COMMERCE

1

GREATER MINNEAPOLIS
CHAMBER OF COMMERCE

2

INDIGOPOOL.com

3

RZB
Group

4

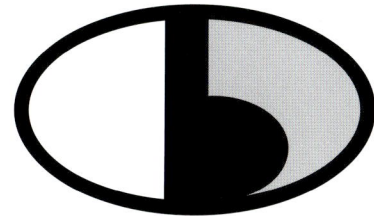

GAB
Robins®

5

BARKERS

6

San Juan
Bautista
Chamber of Commerce

7

Orange County
HOMES & LOANS

1

**New York City
Economic Development
Corporation**

2

The Loan
CORPORATION

3

Stellar
Financial Systems Inc.

4

5

New City
MORTGAGE LLC

6

STARS AND STRIPES
INTERNATIONAL

7

1
ORANGE COUNTY HOMES AND LO-
ANS

2
NEW YORK CITY ECONOMIC DEV-
ELOPMENT CORPORATION

3
THE LOAN CORPORATION

4
STELLAR FINANCIAL SYSTEMS
INC.

5
WHITEHALL CAPITAL

6
NEW CITY MORTGAGE LLC

7
STARS AND STRIPES INTERNATI-
ONAL

1
BENJAMIN FISHER

2
ALLEY CAPITAL PARTNERS LLC

3
INDEPENDENT

4
WILMINGTON TRUST

5
AMERICAN CENTURY

6
FUTURES ONLINE

7
POWER TRACK

1

2

3

4

5

6

7

Thomson Financial™
ACTIVE EXPRESS®

1

Big Charts™

2

ANALYST TOOL™
A PRODUCT OF DISCLOSURE INCORPORATED

5

Financial Network

3

6

USA LOAN®

4

Northwestern Mutual
FINANCIAL NETWORK™

7

1
THOMSON FINANCIAL ACTIVE EX-
PRESS

2
BIG CHARTS

3
FINANCIAL NETWORK

4
USA LOAN

5
ANALYST TOOL

6
THYSSENKRUPP

7
NORTHWESTERN MUTUAL FINANC-
IAL NETWORK

1
FIDELITY INVESTMENTS

2
CAPITAL ACCESS

3
ARONOFF CENTER

4
TREASURY CONNECT

5
STRATEGIC ACCOUTS

6
BENEFICIAL

7
CLARICA

1

2

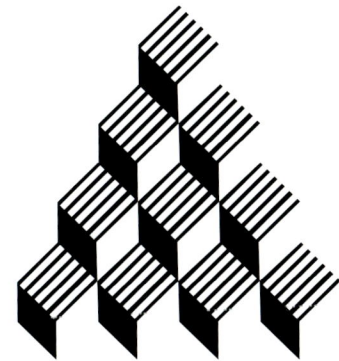

5

3

6

4

7

Saudi American Bank
World Class Banking
1

First World International Bank
2

GarantiBank
6

BANQUE DE FINANCIER
BANK OF FINANCE
3

citigroup
7

Banca Ţiriac
4

CIB
BANK
Gruppo IntesaBci
8

YAPI KREDi
5

1
UNIVERSITY FEDERAL SAVINGS
& LOAN

2
SRPSKA REGIONLNA BANKA
SRB

3
BANKS

4
MINAMI OSAKA SHINYO KINKO

5
PROVIDIAN FINANCIAL

6
FLEET

7
VIRTUAL BANK

8
NIKOIL INVESTMENT BANKING
GROUP

9
STANDARD BANK LONDON

1

6

SRB

srpska regionalna banka

2

VirtualBank

7

Banks

3

4

NIKOIL

INVESTMENT BANKING GROUP

8

PROVIDIAN

Financial

5

Standard Bank London

9

1

مصرف أبوظبي للإسلامي
Abu Dhabi Islamic Bank

2

3

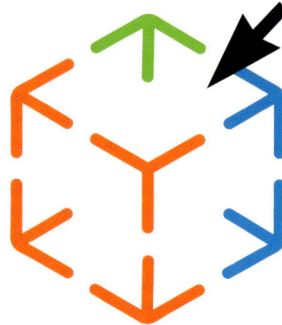

4

5

6

7

NewFrontierBank
At home in St. Charles County

8

1
BANCO DE LTALIA. BUENOS AIRES

2
ABU DHABI ISLAMIC BANK

3
CHEMICAL BANK

4
COMMERCE BANK
Comm-erce

5
RPM

6
CORPORATE CONCEPTS-PBS

7
TAI SHIN INTERNATIONAL BANK

8
NEW FRONTIER BANK

1
COMMUNITY STATE BANK

2
NATIONAL BANK OF DUBAI

3
CAL FED

4
EUREKA BANK

5
CITY NATIONAL BANK THE WAY UP

6
THE EQUITY EDGE

7
COMMERZ BANK

8
IMPERIAL BANCORP

1

2

3

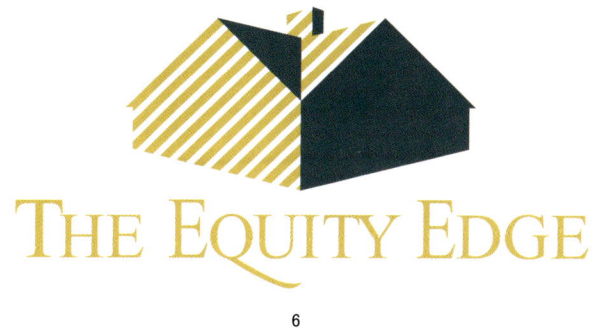

4

5

6

7

8

1ST INTRANET BANK
NORTH AMERICA

1

SMBC

2

Achieve
anything.

3

VISA

4

Bank of America.

5

CHASE

6

7

DeutscheBank

8

1
CORPORATE CONCEPTS-PBS

2
SUMITOMO MITSUI BANKING
CORPORATION

3
KEY BANK

4
VISA

5
BANK OF AMERICA

6
CHASE

7
FRONTIER FARM CREDIT

8
DEUTSCHE BANK

1
HANA BANK

2
HYOGO SHINKIN BANK

3
SAN DIEGO NATIONAL BANK

4
ТРАНCКРЕINTБAHK

5
THE OITA BANK

6
APRISA/NORTHWESTBANK

7
BUSINESS BANK OF AMEICAN

8
BANCO ESPIRITO SANTO

Hana Bank
1

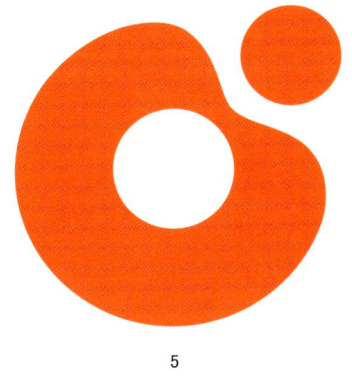
5

HYOSHIN
2

aprisa
6

San Diego National Bank
3

7

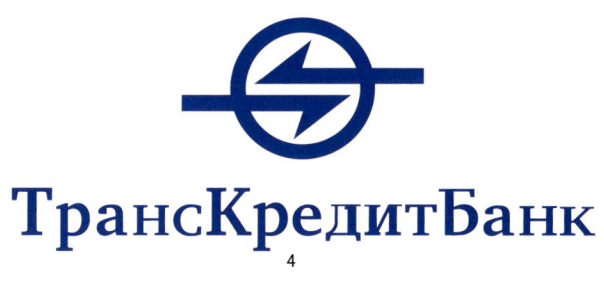
ТрансКредитБанк
4

BANCO ESPIRITO SANTO
8

1
FLEET

2
SOUTHERN FLORIDA BANK

3
THE ROYAL BANK OF SCOTLAND
GROUP

4
JEFFERIES

5
BANK WEST

6
ORANGE COUNTY'S CREDIT UNION

7
RENTEN BANK

8
ROYAL BANK OF CANADA

1
SIGNAL BANK

2
BLOM BANK

3
TREASURY UNITED STATES MINT

4
HONG KONG MEVAS BANK

5
GRUPPO INTESABCI

6
THE PFANDBRIEF

7
SHINHAN BANK

MEVASBank

4

SIGNAL

BANK

1

Gruppo IntesaBci

5

BLOM BANK

Peace of Mind

2

THE PFANDBRIEF

issued by Germany's mortgage banks

6

UNITED STATES MINT

3

Shinhan Bank

7

189

NJFAM LY CARE

1

2

5

6

Healthcare *for* Women

3

ViaCord

Featuring unconventional sound adventures and daring endeavors in new instrumental music.

4

7

4

1
LIFENET HEALTH PLANS

2
IRS AIMS

3
WORKWELL

4
LONGVIEW

5
AETNA

6
CAREMARK

7
AFLAC

1

5

2

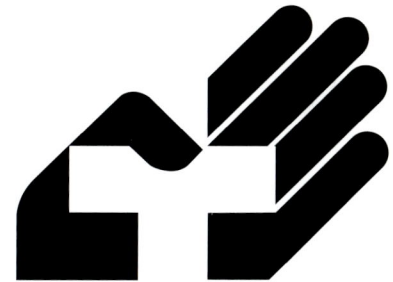

6

3

7

191

1

2

APRIA HEALTHCARE

3

DiPrima
Insurance Specialists

4

Cardinal Health

5

L·I·F·E

MANAGER

6

Insurance
Education
Corporation

7

James River
Mortgage LLC

8

1
TELESIS HEALTH CARE

2
HEALTH PROM

3
APRIA HEALTHCARE

4
DIPRIMA INSURANCE SPECIALIS-
TS

5
CARDINAL HEALTH

6
NATIONWIDE INSURANCE

7
THE INSURANCE EDUCATION COR-
PORATION

8
JAMES RIVER MORTGAGE LLC

1
L.A.CARE

2
NATIONAL TRAVELERS LIFE

3
NFIP

4
KEMPER INSURANCE COMPANIES

5
SYNAPSE CO

6
SUN LIFE FINANCIAL

7
HEALTH EXTRAS

L.A. Care
HEALTH PLAN

1

Kemper®
Insurance Companies

4

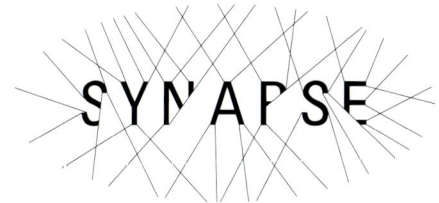

SYNAPSE

5

EXPO '97

2

Sun
Life Financial SM

6

National Flood Insurance Program
NFIP
Administered by FEMA

3

HEALTHEXTRAS

7

CONSECO

1

2

Foundation Health Systems, Inc.

3

5

6

Lincoln Heritage
LIFE INSURANCE COMPANY

4

7

1
CONSECO

2
MEDCO HEALTH

3
FHS

4
LINCOLN HERITAGE LIFE INSUR-
ANCE COMPANY

5
OXFOED HEALTH PLANS

6
CIGNA

7
NATIONWIDE INSURANCE

1
VHA

2
MEASURISK.COM

3
UNIVERSAL HEALTH NETWORK

4
SETTLEMENT HEALTH

5
GUARDIAN

6
LIFE EQUITY LLC

7
HOMEWOOD CORPORATION

8
WHOLE HEALTH MANAGEMENT INC

1

2

3

4

5

6

7

8

Telcom

1

5

2

3

6

4

7

1
E SURANCE.COM

2
AUSTRALIAN MEDICAL ENTERPRI-
SE HEALTHCARE

3
FUTURE ONE

4
HUMANA

5
INSURANCE QUALITY MARK

6
TRAVELERS

7
HEALTHTRAC

8
GENTIVA HEALTH SERVICES

1

5

2

6

3

7

4

8

1

2

3

Instinet

A REUTERS Company

4

5

6

7

8

1
MERRILL LYNCH

2
EQUIBOND

3
THE AMERICAN STOCK EXCHANGE

4
GLOBAL TRADE PARTNERS

5
DATEK ONLINE

6
SWISS EXCHANGE

7
WACHOVIA SECURITIES

8
AMERITRADE

1

5

2

6

3

7

4

8

1

5

1
BIG HEN MANAGEMENT LTD

2
THE EDUCATION PLAN

3
BRIDEWAY CAPITAL

4
KIERNAN VENTURES

5
NEW WORLD CHINA

6
VALUE LINE

7
TONE YEE INVESTMENTS & DEVE-
LOPMENTS

2

3

6

4

7

1
FAIRHAVEN PARTNERS INVESTME-
NT GROUP

2
MANNING & NAPIER

3
FANNIE MAE

4
THE MONY GROUP

5
B.C.ZIEGLER AND COMPANY

6
VENTURESTAR

7
PIONEER

8
THOMAS WEISEL PARTNERS

1

5

2

6

3

7

4

8

1

5

2

6

3

7

SANTA BARBARA TECHNOLOGY INCUBATOR, LLC

4

8

1
360 INVESTMENTS

2
LIBERTY MUTUAL

3
GEEN TREE LENDING GROUP

4
SANTA BARBARA TECHNOLOGY IN-
CUBATOR.LLC

5
WEST LB

6
WILLOW INVESTING

7
ALLIANCE CAPITAL

8
BARES CAPITAL

1
TERRA FIRMA

2
PARTECH INTERNATIONAL

3
PIONEER INVESTMENTS

4
SHAWMUT CAPITAL

5
JOHN HANCOCK FUNDS

6
CHASE FUNDS

7
EQUITY SOURCE

TERRA FIRMA
real estate Investments, LLC.

1

4

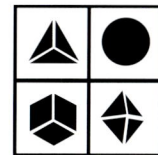

JOHN HANCOCK FUNDS
A Global Inveestment Management Firm

5

P A R T E C H
I N T E R N A T I O N A L

2

CHASE FUNDS

6

PIONEER
Investments®

3

EquitySource
Innovative Capital Creation

7

M.A. Weatherbie & Co., Inc.

1

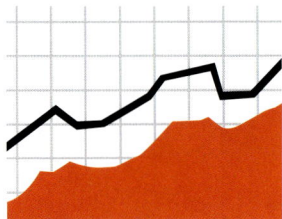

PERFORMANCE
CAPITAL GROUP, L.L.C.

2

ANGEL FIRE™

3

WAUSAU

4

INSURANCE & INVESTMENT

5

cFour Partners
A Partner Firm of ITP Worldwide

6

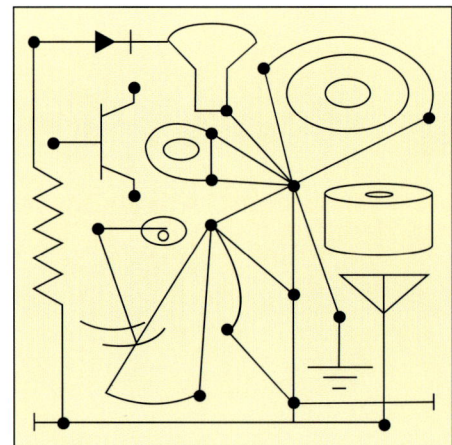

7

1
M.A. WEATHERBIE & CO.,INC

2
PERFORMANCE CAPITAL GROUP/K-IRKKELLOGG

3
ANGEL FIRE

4
WAUSAU MEMBER OF LIBERTY M-UTUAL GROUP

5
AXA

6
CFOUR PARTNERS

7
INFORMATION TECHNOLOGY VEN-

1
SPROUT GROUP

2
NEW WEALTH FUNDS

3
PRINCE INVESTMENTS

4
STREETSIDE INVESTORS

5
WOODLAND INVESTMENT. CO

6
BAIA INVESTORS GROUP . INC

7
STRONG VALUE GROUP

1

STREETSIDE INVESTOR

4

NewWealth
FUNDS

2

5

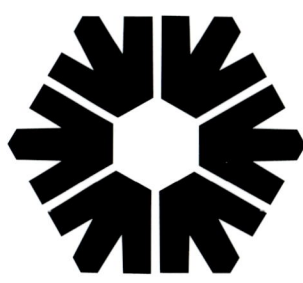

Baia
investors group, inc.

6

PRINCE
INVESTMENTS

3

STRONG
VALUE GROUP

7

205

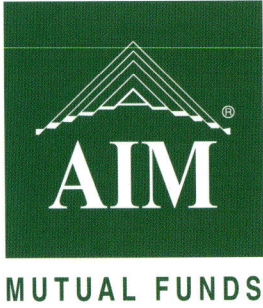

MUTUAL FUNDS

1

INVESTMENT MANAGEMENT

5

General Altantic Partners

2

6

3

7

4

8

1
AIM

2
GENERAL ALTANTIC PARTNERS

3
CAPITAL STREAM

4
HELIE GROUPE FINANCIER

5
MFS

6
WIT CAPITAL

7
FANNIE MAE

8
STOCK BRIDGE CAPITAL

1
CHRISTOPHER STREET

2
HAMMERQUIST & HALVERSON

3
CORBIS

4
FLYCAST NETWORK

5
ACTIVE MOTIF

6
NEUFELDT'S

7
DIESEL

1

4

ACTIVE MOTIF

5

2

6

Corbis®

3

DIESEL DESIGN

7

1

2

3

4

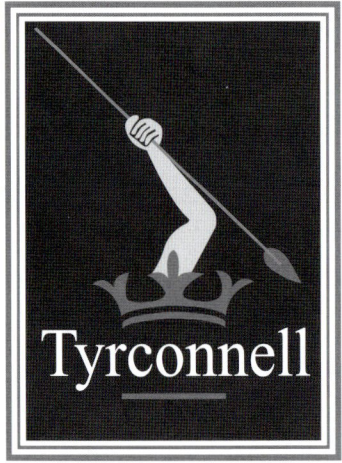

5

6

7

1
THE DESIGN AGENCY

2
AD OUTLET.COM

3
ELEMENT GROUP

4
BEYOND INTERACTIVE

5
KICK FIRE

6
TYRCONNELL

7
BE

1
WORK,INC.

2
TACH

3
PACESETTER

4
"S" —TEAM

5
AD FORCE

6
DESIGN DIMENSION INC

7
LBJFKKK

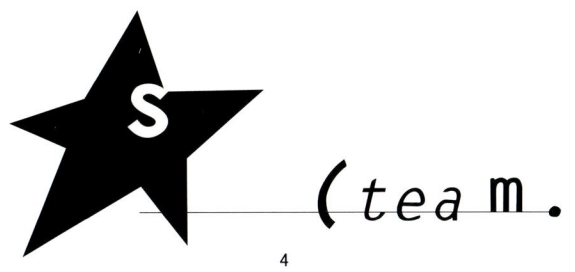

4

1

5

2

6

3

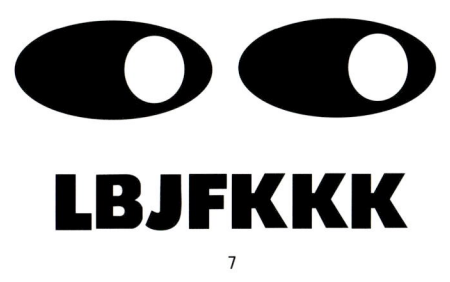

7

Advertising.com sm

1

CARPE DATUM

2

3

BUSINESS IMAGE®

4

RICEREE

5

6

7

1
ADVERTISING.COM

2
CARPE DATUM

3
JULIE GUSTAFSON WORDS THAT WORK

4
BUSINESS IMAGE

5
RICEREE

6
TALKING HAED

7
MIAMI-FT.LAUDERDALE INTERCONNECT

1
RKS DESIGN INC

2
SQUARE D

3
DIVIDEND

4
CAHNERS

5
CYNTRIC

6
DATA CREATIVE INC

7
JIM DICKINSON

8
ADVERB

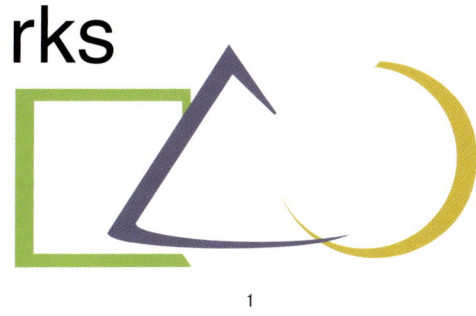

1

CYNTRIC

5

2

DATA CREATIVE INC.

6

3

7

Cahners

4

ad Verb

8

AdOutlet

1

2

3

4

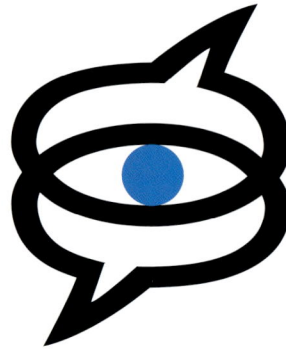

5

6

7

1
TRI ACTIVE.INC.

2
EYE WIRE

3
XOW!

4
ART TUROCK & ASSOCIATES

5
ADSMART

6
CATHEY ASSOCIATES.INC

7
THE VISUAL GROUP

4

1

5

2

6

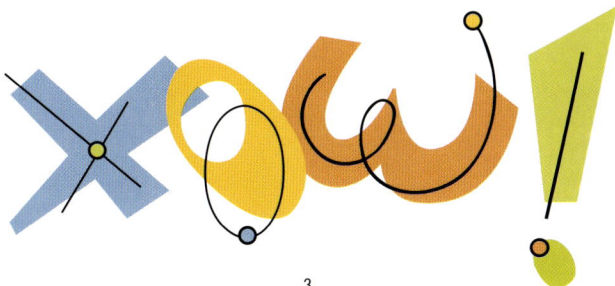

3

7

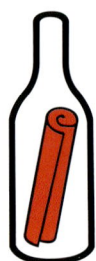

Digeno

AN RR DONNELLEY COMPANY

1

Bonaire

Parque Comercial y de Ocio

2

INTERACTIVE

M**Y**NDS

3

Vubox

4

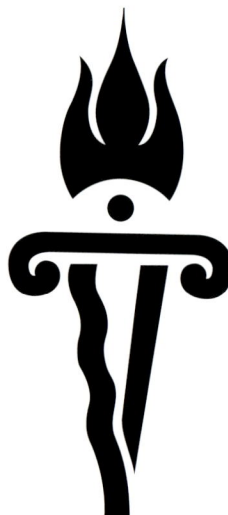

5

6

z o o p e r

7

1
RR DONNELLY & SONS
Digeno

2
GRUPO RIOFISA

3
INTERACTIVE MINDS

4
VUBOX

5
WINNING VISIONS

6
MADE ON EARTH

7
ZOOPER

1
MEDIA TEMPLE

2
GARDNER DESIGN

3
TODO MUNDO

4
TEE SHIRT COMPANY

5
THE DANDY CANDY MAN

6
MATTHEW BENDER

7
WORK.INC.

1

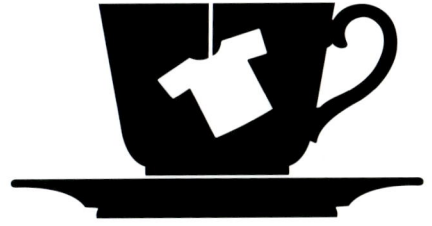

4

5

2

6

3

7

215

1

2

F I S H E R

3

e a s t 3

4

5

6

invision design
GEORGOPULOS

7

8

1
L90 INTERNET ADVERTISING SO-
LUTIONS

2
META CREATIONS

3
FISHER

4
EAST 3

5
THINK

6
D.F.King

7
INVISION DESIGN GEORGOPULOS

8
ADS

1
CHRIS GRAY

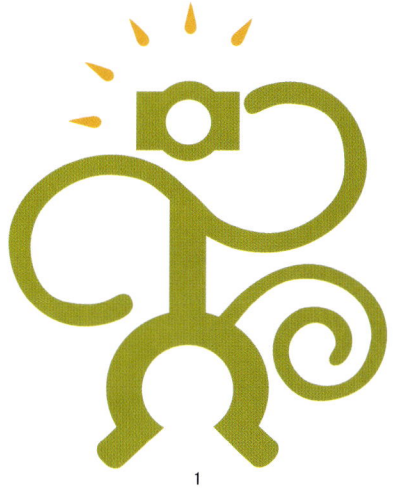

2
KELLEEN GRIFFIN

3
MADE ON EARTH

4
JERRY COWART DESIGNERS

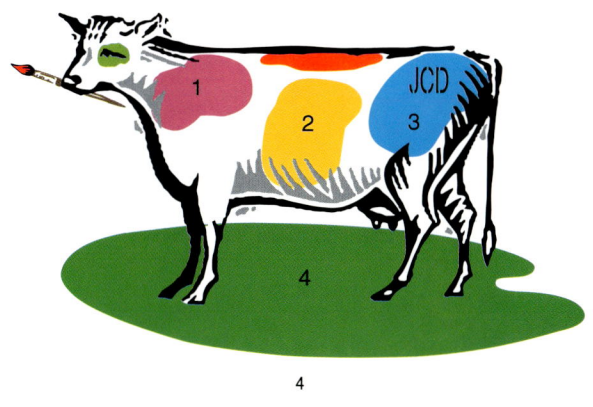

5
MACHADO & ASSOCIATES

6
TECHNICALLY CORRECT COPYWRI-
TING

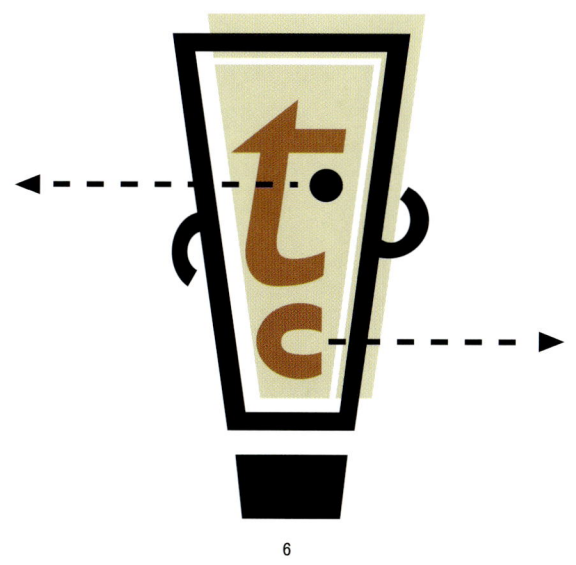

1

4

2

Machado & Associates

A D V E R T I S I N G

5

3

6

American Minorities Media

1

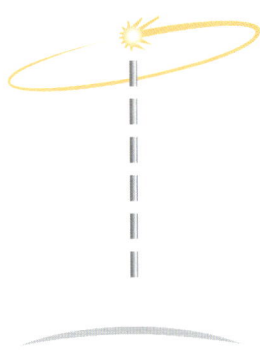

VECTIS
Group

2

The Color People

3

Eyeball™.com

4

I N V E N T A

5

r | e | d +M

6

MILLENNIUM ADVERTISING

7

DIGITAL SAVANT

8

1
AMERICAN MINORITIES MEDIA

2
VECTIS GROUP

3
THE COLOR PEOPLE

4
EYEBALL.COM

5
INVENTA INC

6
R E D + M

7
MILLENNIUM ADVERTISING

8
DIGITAL SAVANT

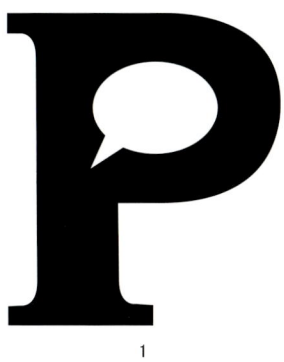

1

4

5

2

6

3

7

1

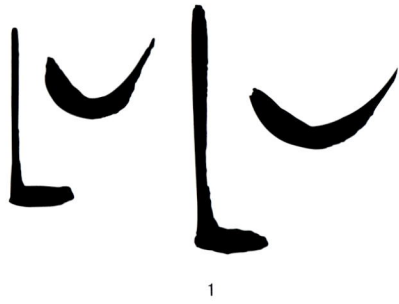

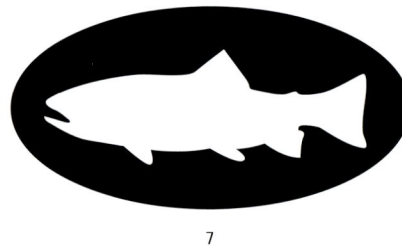

5

2

6

3

7

4

BONDI

8

1
JOSEPH WU ORIGAMI INC

2
MORRIS CREATIVE

3
ENTERPINSE IRELAND

4
DOGSTAR

5
RADIO VISION INTERNATIONAL

6
PLUG & PLAY READY DOWNTOWN DE-
NVER

7
B-THERE.COM

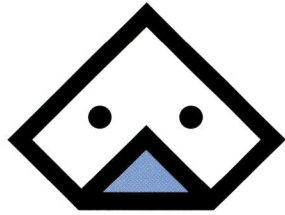

JOSEPH WU
ORIGAMI INC
1

MORRIS
CREATIVE
2

ENTERPINSE
IRELAND
3

PAST DUE
4

5

Plug & Play
Ready
6

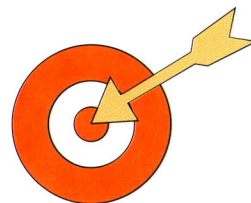

b-there.com
7

221

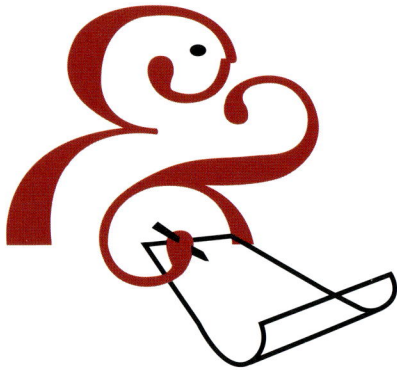

1

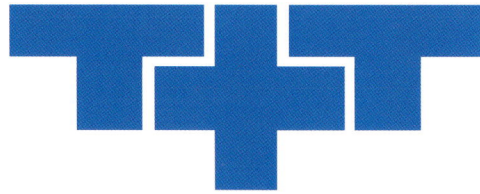

5

2

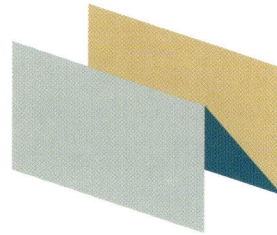

NOTEWORTHY

6

3

terapin

4

WETDAWG

7

BERLIN PACKAGING "PINNACLE"

1

tom biondic
graphic designer
ideas for everyone

2

SOUL

3

STARWAVE

4

UNITY

5

ashleyballard

6

7

1
THE CREATIVE CIRCUS

2
TOM BIONDIC GRAPHIC DESIGNER

3
SOUL

4
STAR WAVE

5
UNITY

6
ASHLEY BALLARD

7
DEEP 6

1
FRASEWORKS

2
PANGEA

3
DESIGN GROUP

4
THE ONE ESSENTIAL ITEM

5
CRIMM DESIGN

6
ROYAL GRAPHICS

7
PHILLIPS DESIGN

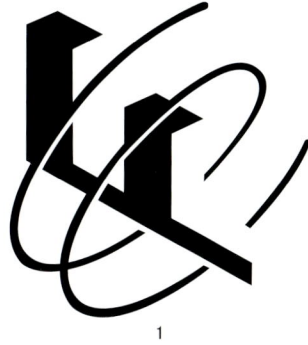

1

2

3

4

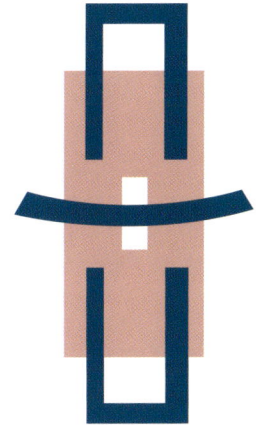

5

6

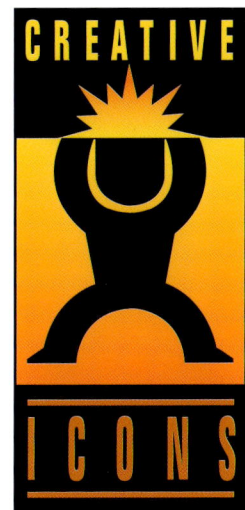

7

maak1

1

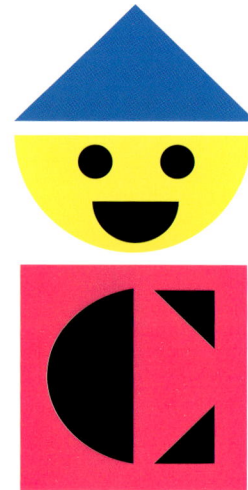

TropicalHomes

2

3

HALO Innovations, Inc.

4

1
MAAK1

2
TROPICAL HOMES

3
CHRISTINE'S 20TH CENTURY F-
URNISHINGS

4
HALO INNOVATIONS,INC

5
COLOR FORM

6
ROSE LINK

7
POWER HOUSE DESIGNS

5

RoseLink

6

PowerHouse

7

1
IRIS INTERNET

2
C.SHOEMAKER

3
FRED WILKERSON

4
CREST GRAPHICS.INC.

5
THE LOGO CHEF

6
CHICAGO 27 DESIGNERS

7
WILER FONG ASSOCIATES

8
ITM CREATIONS

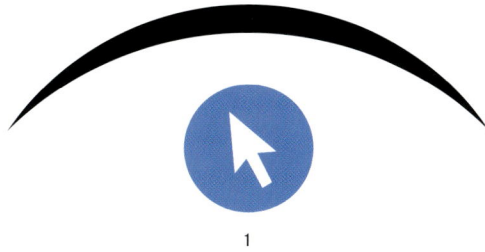

1

C_SHOEMAKER

2

3

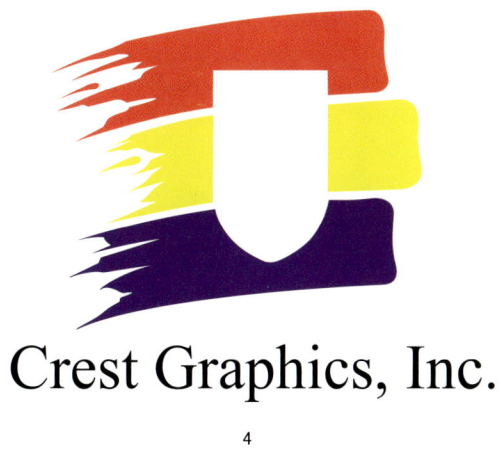

Crest Graphics, Inc.

4

THE logochef

5

6

Think outside.

7

ITM
CREATIONS

8

1

2

3

4

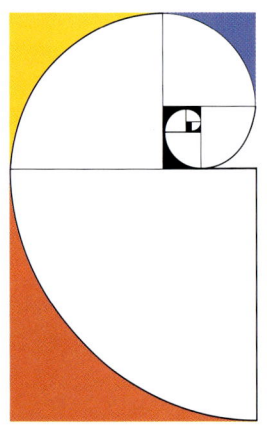

5

6

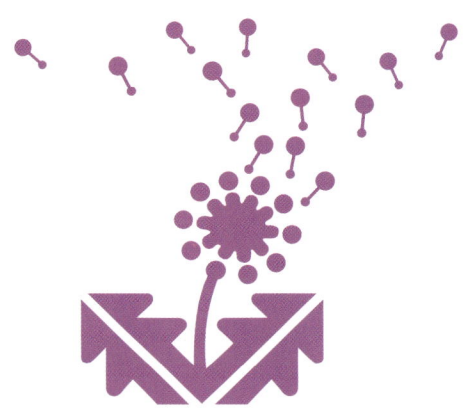

7

1
WORLD INTERATIVE

2
MONKEY STUDIOS

3
PREJEAN LOBUE CREATIVE WORKS

4
RICH HENDERSON

5
GSH DESIGN

6
PETER GEISS

7
BARUNSON FANCY CO.,LTD

1
FORWARD DESIGN

2
RICH SCHAEFER

3
VAUGHN WILLIAMS

4
XTENSIBLE DESIGN

5
MOW TOWN

6
STUDIO INTERNATIONAL

7
INNOVATION

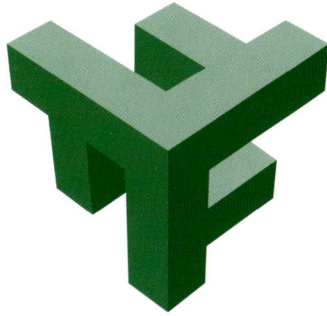

1

Xtensible Design

4

MOWTOWN
COMMERCIAL & RESIDENTIAL LAWN SERVICE

5

2

6

3

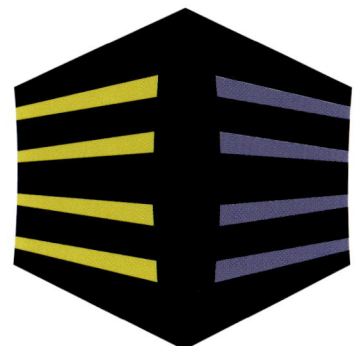

7

1

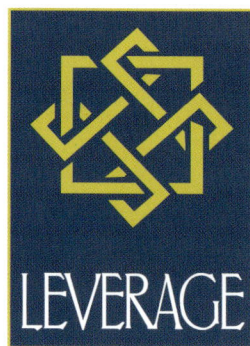
2

3

RED FINE HORSE
4

LEVERAGE
5

6

7

Cultivations™
Home · Garden · Life
8

1
TOP GRAPHICS

2
STE

3
HERMAN MILLER

4
RED FINE HORSE

5
LEVERAGE STUDIO

6
JAZZA

7
WESLI MANCINI FABRIC DESIGN

8
CULTIVATIONS

1
QV DESIGN

2
BASKETS BY DESIGN

3
MUZAK

4
ALIMENTERICS INC

5
BACK YARD DESIGN

6
BUZ DESIGN GROUP

7
LAND EXPRESSIONS

DESIGN

1

baskets
BY DESIGN

2

3

4

5

6

LAND
EXPRESSIONS LLC

7

Bansai
萬菜

1

Jeff maul

2

BEALS MARTIN

3

SIERRA DESIGNS

4

William Morrow and Associates

5

6

WORK

7

1
PAT FOSS

2
JEFF MAUL

3
BEALS MARTIN

4
SIERRA DESIGNS

5
WILLIAM MORROW AND ASSOCIATES

6
DESIGN TRIBE

7
WORK.LNC

1
PERSONAL COMMUNICATIONS INT-
ERACTIVE

2
SPROUTS DESIGN

3
PACIFIC GRAPHICS

4
BURO HAPPOLD

5
STEFAN DZIALLAS

6
CRAMER CALLIGRAPHY

7
SPECTRUM DESIGN

8
WERT

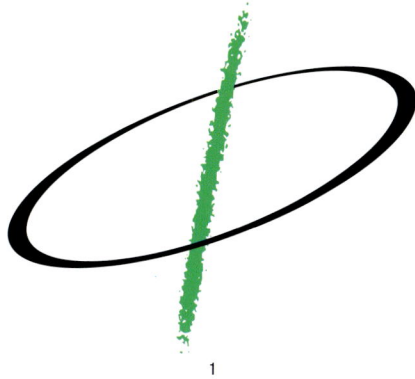

1

5

2

6

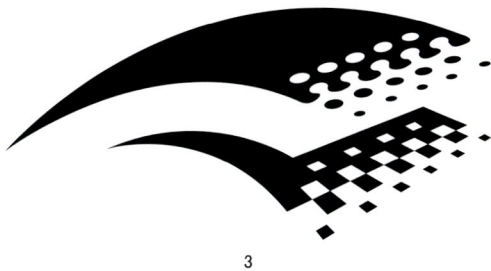

3

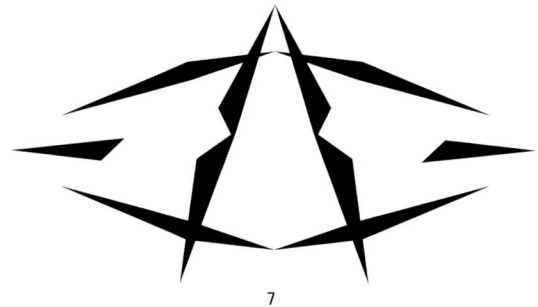

7

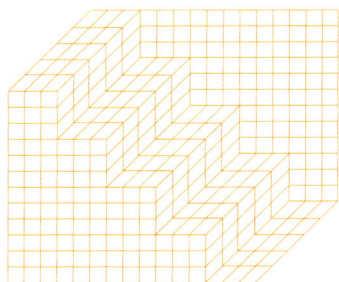

Buro Happold

4

Wert
C O M P A N Y
I N C.

8

1

2

6

CURRY

3

5

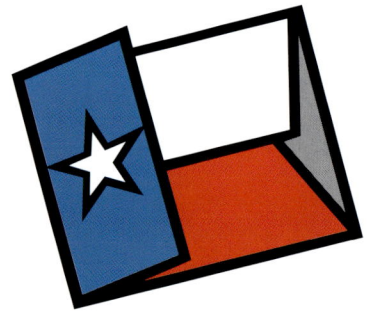

7

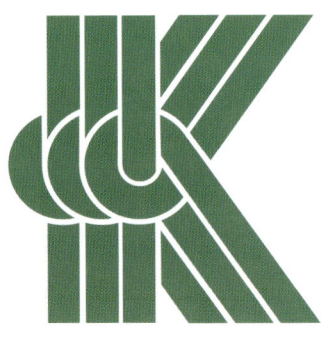

4

TWI

8

1
GRAPHIC ARTISTS GUILD

2
CLAY ADAMS

3
CURRY GRAPHICS-SILK SCREEN

4
PAT JENKINS

5
MICKY WISON

6
HEIDELBERG

7
PARIS PACKAGING

8
TWI

1
GRAVES FOWLER ASSOCIATES

2
MADE ON EARTH

3
ZAPF

4
KELLEHER DESIGN

5
J.EITING&CO.

6
CODA CREATIVE INC.

7
BRAINSTORM DESIGN

8
INTERNET ADVERTISING BUREAU

g:f
graves fowler associates
1

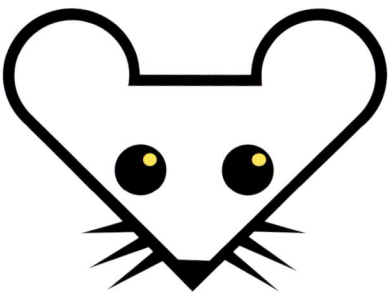

2

5

Zapf Creation®
3

CODA CREATIVE inc.
6

4

On
7

internet advertising bureau
8

1

5

2

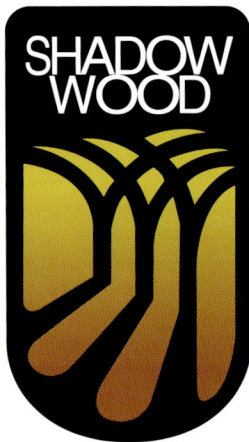

3

6

4

7

1
INNO DESIGN

2
INSITE DESIGN INC

3
EVENT DESIGN

4
EVOLVE

5
BILL ROLLE & ASSOCIATES

6
CAROL & KANDA

7
JEFF STEPHENS

INNODESIGN

1

5

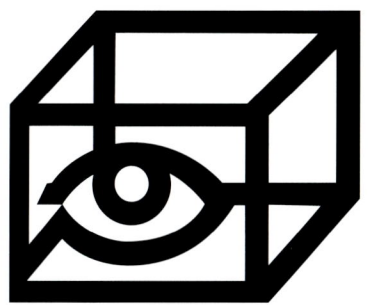

2

6

EVENT DESIGN

3

Evolve.

4

7

1

2

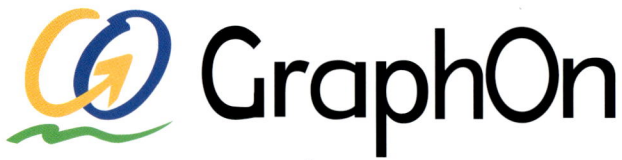

veenendaal**cave**

3

F L E U R Y

D E S I G N

4

Gray Cat

GRAPHIC DESIGN

5

6

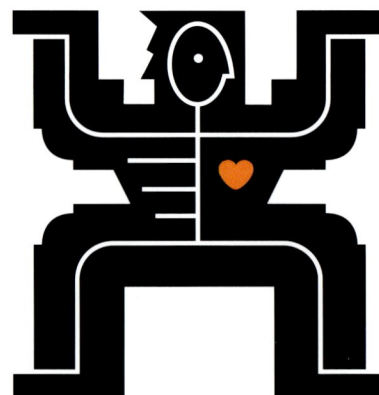

7

1
AIGA—ECOLOGY OF DESIGN

2
GRAPH ON

3
VEENENDAALCAVE

4
FLEURY DESIGN

5
GRAY CAT GRAPHIC DESIGN

6
DESIGN LAB

7
CHARLES JAMES

1
BAILEY DESIGN GROUP.INC

2
THINKSTREAM

3
DREW MORRISON

4
LIFESCAN

5
FINE DESIGN GROUP

6
TRICKETT & WEBB

7
LUCILLE & HENRY HOME TEXTILES

8
LORET CARBONE

bailey design group inc

1

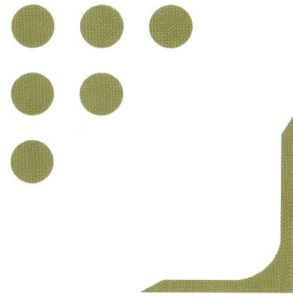

5

6

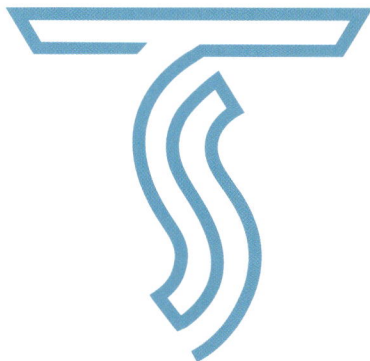

2

3

Lucille & Henry
Home Textiles

7

4

8

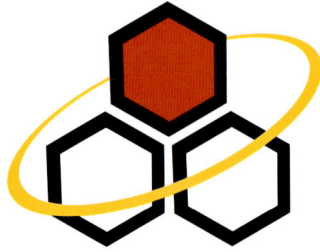

1

HARPER
WHERE YOUR IMAGE IS EVERYTHING.

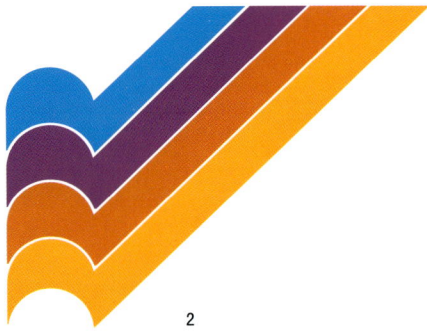

2

3

4

IMPROVED
PACKAGING

5

6

7

8

1
HARPER

2
MARLO GRAPHICS INC

3
BLACK RHINO GRAPHIS

4
VILLE LA REINE

5
INLAND PAPERBOARD & PACKAG-
ING.INC

6
PUNCH

7
RONALD EMMERLING DESIGN .INC

8
CONCEPT UNLIMITED.INC.

1
DEER

2
BRAIN

3
CUSTOM BINDER LINE

4
FLYING TIGER

5
212 DESIGN INC.

6
GIFTED.LTD

7
DEREK YEE DESIGN

1

4

5

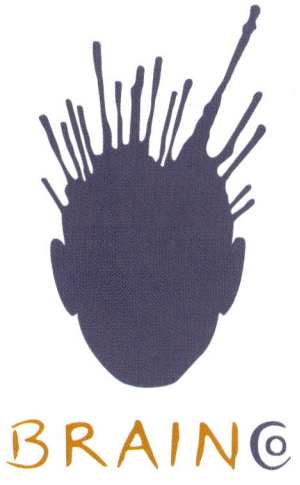

2

6

7

3

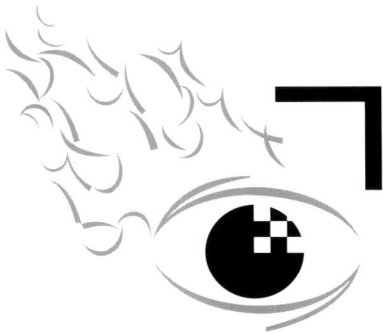

1

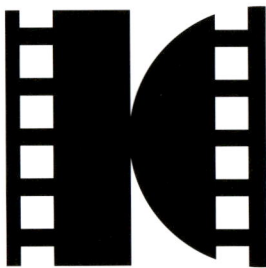

2

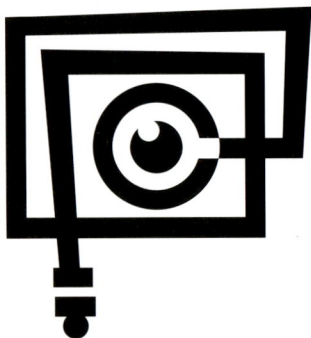

3

4

5

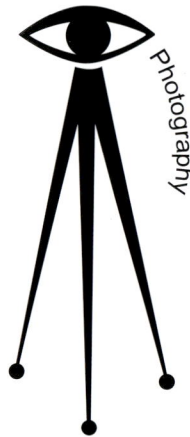

6

7

1
MODE

2
PHOTO FUSION

3
KIM COOPER

4
PAUL CHAUNCEY PHOTOGRAPHY

5
LESLI BARTON PHOTOGRAPHY

6
ANDREW TAMERIUS PHOTOGRAPHY

7
JOHN CROWE PHOTOGRAPHY

1
MAX PHOTOGRAPHY

2
EYE LIKE

3
THE PICTURE PEOPLE

4
JOE PHOTO

5
BARRY GORDIN PHOTOGRAPHY

6
MICHAEL BONE PHOTOGRAPHY

7
ANDREW HUNT PHOTOGRAPHY

8
MAD COW STUDIO

1

5

2

6

3

7

4

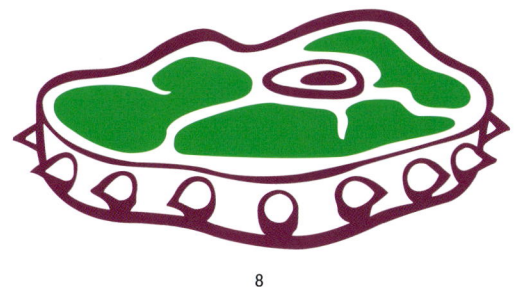

8

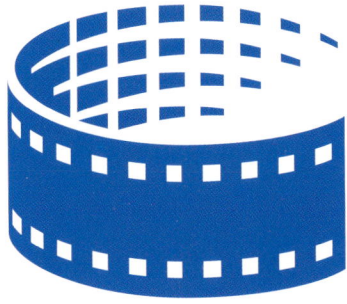

1

2

3

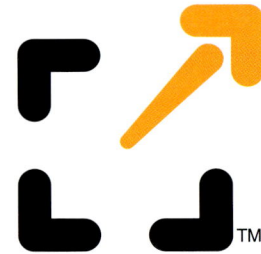

4

5

6

7

8

1
SPECTRUM PHOTOGRAPHIC

2
RICK KOOKER PHOTOGRAPHY

3
KIRK WORDEN PHOTOGRAPHY

4
ELIZABETH ZESCHIN PHOTOGRAPHY

5
RIGHT VIEW PRO

6
DEFINITIVE STOCK

7
CREATIVE MEMORIES

8
TREASURED MOMENTS

1
CARTÍ SCULPTURES

2
KLIK

3
MASTERFILE

4
OPTI SYSTEMS

5
THE STOCK MARKET

6
THE BLACK BOOK

7
PHOTO 2000

8
PHOTO DISC

1

5

2

6

3

7

4

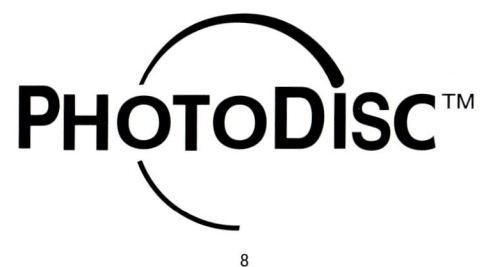

8

IMAGICOMM

1

SPD
PHOTOGRAPHY

2

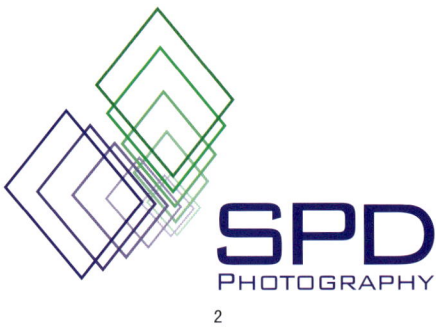

3

PIX

4

5

6

SHARPSHOOTERS

7

Giga Pixel

8

1
IMAGICOMM INSPIRATIONAL NET-
WORK

2
SPD PHOTOGRAPHY

3
STEVE MARSEL STUDIO

4
PIX

5
PHOTO EFFECTS

6
HEATHER SWANNER, FIGURE PHO-
TOGRAPHER

7
SHARPSHOOTERS

8
GIGA PIXEL

1
SOCIETY FOR TECHNICAL COMM-
UNICATION CONFERENCE

2
WWW.TRYSCIENCE.ORG

3
@D:TECH

4
PACIFIC TELESIS

5
CHURCHILL CLUB

6
WEALTH MANAGEMENT TECHOLOGY
CONFERENCE

7
ADVERTISING WOMEN OF NEW YORK

8
BMW SOPNSORED SYMOPOSIUM

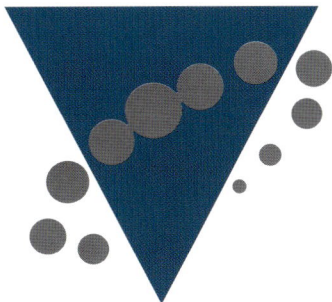

1

2

3

AWNY
ADVERTISING WOMEN OF NEW YORK

7

5

PACIFIC TELESIS
LEADERSHIP 96 | NEW GAMES, NEW RULES

4

6

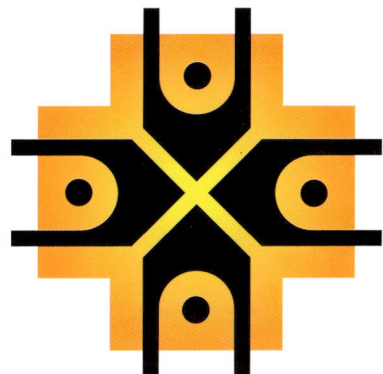

8

Advantage'99
Accelerating Supply Chain Innovations
1

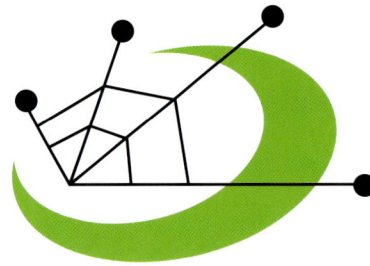

5

BUSINESS2.0
LIVE
MONTEREY 2000
2

TXU
6

National Sleep
2003
AWARENESS WEEK
3

SUMMIT
RECOGNITION PROGRAM
7

healthworld
ENTREPRENEURIAL FORUM
4

8

1
ADVANTAGE'99 ACCELERATING
SUPPLY CHAIN INNOVATIONS

2
"BUSINESS 2.0 LIVE" MONTE-
REY 2000

3
NATIONAL SLEEP AWARENESS WEEK

4
HEALTH WORLD

5
WEB DEVELOPER CONFERENCE 2000

6
TXU

7
SUMMIT RECOGNITION PROGRAM

8
MIT ENTERPRISE FORUM OF CA-
MBRIDGE

1

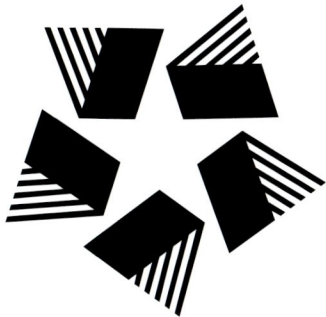

5

2

6

3

7

4

8

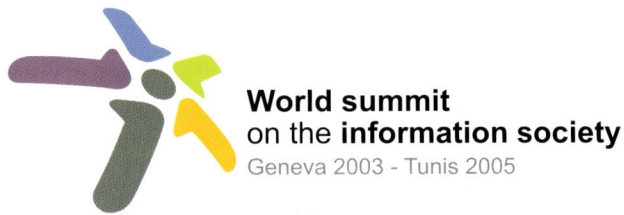

1

5

2

6

3

7

4

8

1
WORLD SUMMIT ON THE INFORM-
ATION SOCIETY

2
INFO WORLD CONFERENCES

3
LIBRARY TELECONFERENCES

4
SEYBOLD

5
NETWORKS FOR BUSINESS NEW
YORK

6
PROFESSIONAL ORGANIZATION
FOR ASSOCIATION EXECUTIVES

7
BUILDING OUR FUTURE/NU SKIN
JAPAN CONVENTION 2001

8
FRIENDS OF CHICAGO RIVER

1
RECHARGE HOPE DAY – BENEFI-
TING INDIVIDUALS WITH JUVE-
NILE ARTHRITIS

2
SBTS MARKET PLACE

3
RUNET 2000

4
YANKEE INVENTION EXPOSITION

5
M & M/TAKEO

6
HERITAGE TRAILS

7
SINGAPORE EXHIBITION & CON-
VENTION BUREAU

8
COW PARADE

1

5

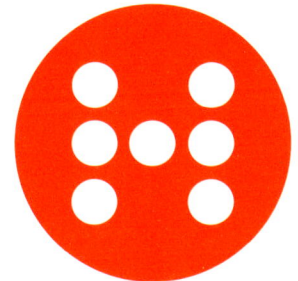

6

2

3

7

4

8

POCKETPC
NEW YORK

1

WINES from
FRANCE

2

5

SOFTWARE
DEVELOPMENT

3

BEST OF
COMDEX
2001

6

COMNET
WASHINGTON, D.C.

4

SPECIAL RISK
DIVISION

7

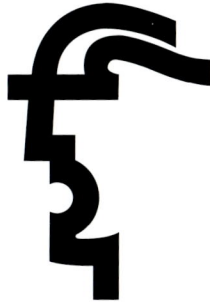

HANNOVER MESSE '98

1

ITU TELECOM WORLD 2003

2

3

TECHXNY

4

radio fair america

5

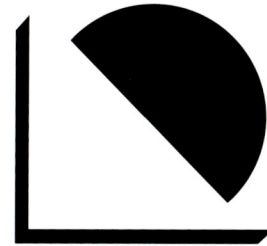

ETRE

6

world light show WLS

7

Parents + KIDS EXPO

8

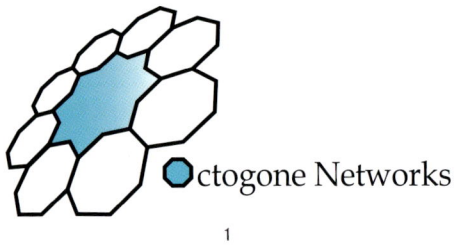

Octogone Networks

1

IQ Networks

2

CONNEXT

3

CONNECT
OHIO

4

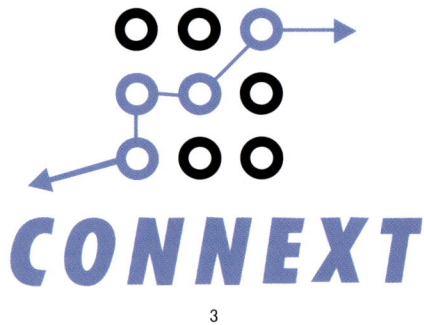

COUNTY
HEALTH
LINK ™

5

AssuredMail

6

THE HEALTH
CONNECTION

7

suplicity

Connect once ● Reach many

8

1
OCTOGONE NETWORKS

2
IQ NETWORKS

3
CONNEXT

4
OHIO

5
COUNTY HEALTH LINK

6
ASSURED MAIL

7
THE HEALTH CONNECTION

8
SUPLICITY

254

1
E DRIVE

2
BLUE CAT NETWORKS

3
COUNTERPANE INTERNET SECURI-
TY

4
CITYWEB

5
SUPLICITY

6
IDNAMES FROM NETWORK SOLUTI-
ONS

7
APAPTEC

8
NETWORK EXPERTS

e-Drive
1

5

idNames™
from NETWORK SOLUTIONS
6

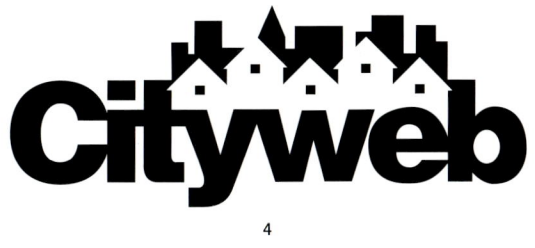

BLUECAT
NETWORKS
2

Counterpane™
Internet Security
3

7

Cityweb
4

Network
EXPERTS
8

255

Minerva Networks

1

BERBEE

5

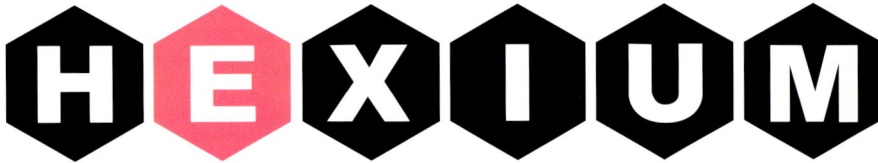

HEXIUM

2

covigo™

3

TNCi

6

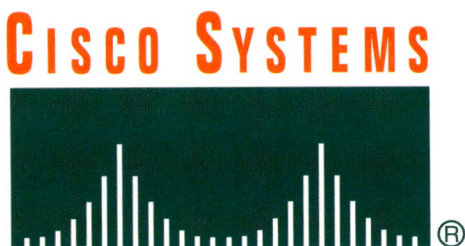

CISCO SYSTEMS

4

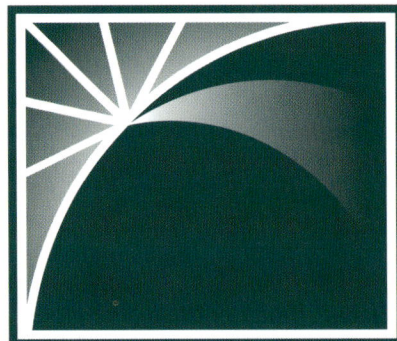

7

1
MINERVA NETWORKS

2
HEXIUM

3
COVIGO

4
CISCO SYSTEMS

5
BERBEE INFORMATION NETWORKS
CORP

6
TNCI

7
TRADELINK AMERICA INC

1
HEARTSEARCH.COM

2
INTERACCESS CORP

3
NET ZERO

4
ORION ATLANTIC

5
BIZ

6
OUR HOUSE

7
VIDEO JUKEBOX NETWORK

8
APPLICAST

1

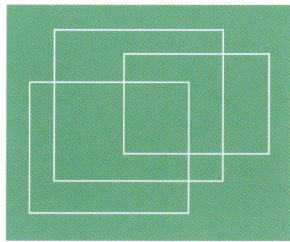
.BIZ ™

5

ourhouse.net

6

2

NetZero

3

JUKEBOX

7

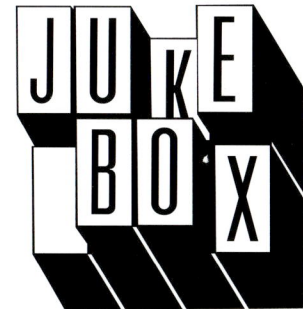
ORION ATLANTIC

4

APPLICAST
Connect Today. Conquer Tomorrow.™

8

1

2

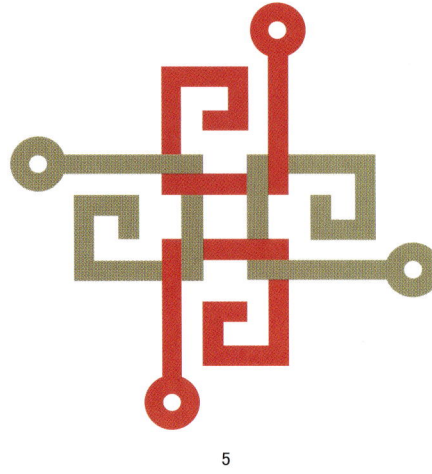

3

4

5

6

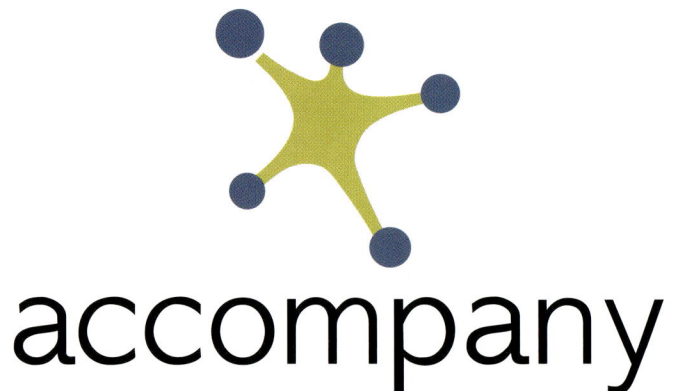

7

1
CHANTRY NETWORKS

2
LWA (LEADING WEB ADVERTISERS)

3
HYPERCOM

4
ACACIA

5
IASIAWORKS INC

6
NET EFFCETS

7
ACCOMPANY

1
NOW

2
DSL

3
VIR LINEAR SWITCH

4
TRAPEZE NETWORKS

5
METASES

6
CISCO

7
ICONOCAST

1

2

3

4

5

6

7

259

LuxN™

1

Aironet™
The ~~Wireless~~ LAN Experts

2

3

network
ASSOCIATES

4

GetThere.com

5

virtual Communities Inc.

6

DCANet

7

NonStopNet

8

1
LUX N

2
AIRONET

3
CISCO

4
NETWORK ASSOCIATES

5
GET THERE.COM

6
VIRTUAL COMMUNITIES INC

7
DCA NET

8
NON STOP NET

1
HEAT.NET PLAY GAMES ONLI-
NE

2
INTERNET SOURCE

3
CNET TELECOMMUNICATIONS

4
MEDIA NETWORKS.INC.

5
FALCON NETWORKS

6
NEW IBIS-INFORMATION NE-
TWORK COMPANY

7
VIA NOVUS

8
PSI NET

HEAT.NET
play games online

1

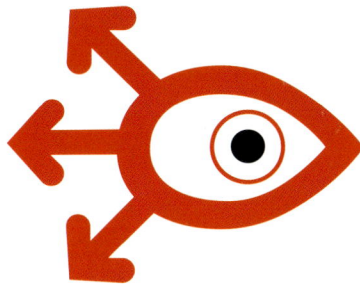

FALCON
NETWORKS

5

INTERNETsource

2

6

CNET

3

VIANOVUS

7

MEDIA NETWORKS.INC.

4

PSINet
Your Internet Business Partner

8

261

1

2

3

6

4

5

7

1
AXIS

2
CIS

3
ACCELERATED NETWORKS

4
CIENA

5
YANTRA

6
OMNI PIN

7
DIGEX

8
JUNO

1

5

2

6

3

7

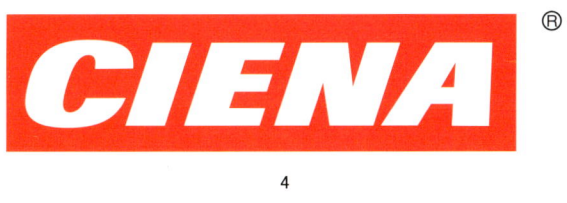

4

8

WEBPARTNER

1

gigabeat™

5

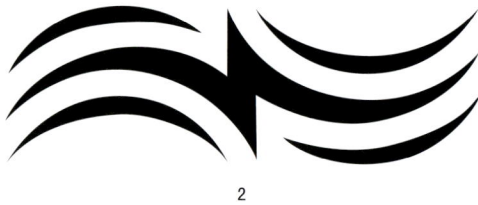

TriNet

3

6

neon

4

EverLink™

7

8

1
WEB PARTNER

2
NETWORK TECHNOLOGY GROUP

3
TRINET HEALTHCARE SYSTEMS

4
NEON

5
GIGABEAT

6
AMAZON.COM

7
EVER LINK

8
DICE COM

1
EXENET

2
GMO

3
NET SUITE

4
AMAZING MAIL.COM

5
CIDERA

6
NAVAHO NETWORKS

7
AJUNTO

8
ICG COMMUNICATIONS

1

5

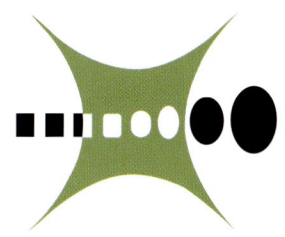

2

6

NETSUITE
ONE SYSTEM. NO LIMITS.

3

Ajunto™

7

4

8

WORLD QUEST
N E T W O R K S

1

NEWBRIDGE

5

homestore.com ™

2

INTERLINK
NETWORKS

3

cypress

6

VIRTUAL
OFFICE

4

HomePage.com

7

1
ATABOK

2
TERASTOR

3
CLICK FOR COTTON

4
EHATCHERY

5
DIGITAL BROADBAND

6
TERAWAVE COMMUNICATIONS

7
NET ZERO.LNC

8
PRONTO NETWORKS

1

5

2

6

3

7

4

8

Sniffer

1

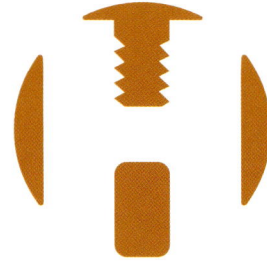

EarthLink

2

3

4

5

6

7

8

1
SNIFFER

2
EARTH LINK

3
AKAMAI

4
3DFX

5
HARDWARE.COM

6
I-LIST CONNECTION

7
MMC NETWORKS

8
INTERNET CAFE

OPEN SESAME

office.com®

1

¡explora!

2

Destina.ca ™ MC

3

planetfeedback

4

Expedia.com®

5

BEAUTYSURG
.com

6

fbr.com sm

7

OBCTV.COM

8

1
OFFICE.COM

2
IEXPLORA!

3
DESTINA.CA

4
PLANET FEEDBACK.COM

5
EXPEDIA.COM

6
BEAUTY SURG.COM

7
FBR.COM

8
OBCTV.COM

1
TRADESHOW.COM

2
AMERICA ONLINE

3
MILITARY.COM

4
SPORTS PAGE.COM

5
BINGO

6
HOTBIZ.COM

7
OCEAN CONNECT.COM

4

1

5

2

6

3

7

271

1

2

3

4

5

6

7

1
CAREERPATH

2
NFL.COM

3
FOOL

4
HIRE ABILITY.COM

5
IPARENTING.COM

6
JUST GIVE.ORG

7
TRAVELOCITY.COM

8
SERVICE9.11.COM

1

iParenting.com

5

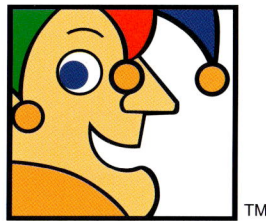

2

Just Give .org

6

Fool.com

3

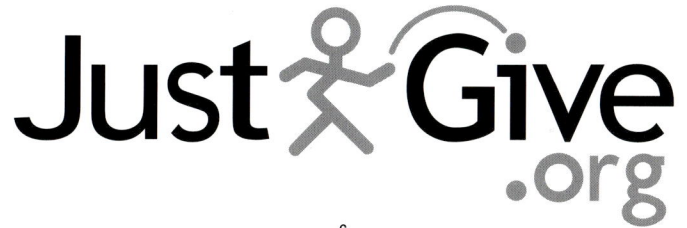

Travelocity.com

7

HireAbility.com

4

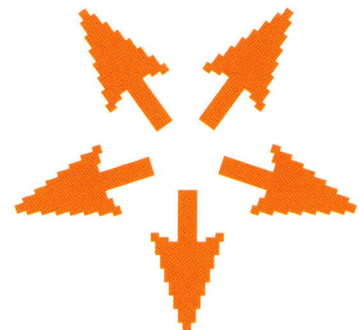

8

1

2

3

CRUEL WORLD

4

formulary kits ONLINE

5

com

6

WhyRunOut.com™

7

PointCast

8

1
PORTABLE LIFE.COM

2
PRODUCE BIZ.COM

3
DE DIAY DE NOCHE

4
POWERIZE.COM

5
VIVIDENCE

6
IWON

7
SILICON OASIS.COM

8
MANAGE.COM

1

5

2

6

3

7

4

8

1

2

3

4

5

6

7

8

1
UK SWISSRUN.COM

2
P2P PLAZA.COM

3
E HOMES OF BAKERSFIELD

4
PHARMANET.COM

5
MBA STAR.COM

6
WORLD SHOPPER.BIZ

7
RIVER CITY GIFTS.COM

8
BIZZ CONNECTION

1
CANADIAN LOBSTER.COM

2
WNBA.COM

3
FLOWER JAR.CO.UK

4
WWW.BOLDCOW.COM

5
EXPRESS PARTY BANNERS.COM

6
CUTE METER

7
E-MAIL-ME.COM

8
WWW.SOBER RECOVERY.COM

CanadianLobster.com
1

5

WNBA.COM
2

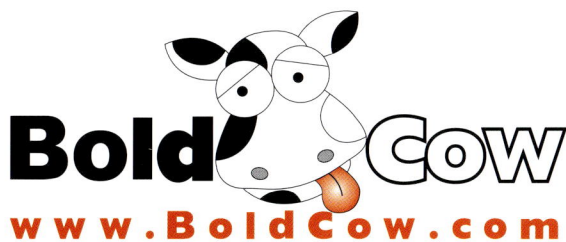
CUTE METER
6

flowerjar .co.uk
Flowers are nice!
3

E-mail-me.com
safe.fast.reliable
7

Bold Cow
www.BoldCow.com
4

www.SoberRecovery.com
Recovery Resources Online
8

1

2

3

4

5

6

7

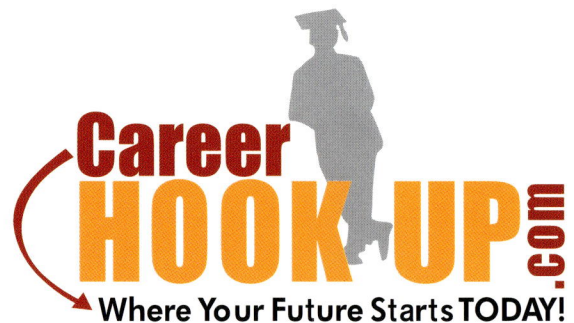

8

1
LIST-CITIES.COM

2
MOVIEPOSTER.COM

3
TRADE WALL STREET

4
THATS NASHVILLE.COM

5
SPEAK-OUT.NET

6
E-SELF.COM

7
PLANETARY NUTRITION.COM

8
CAREER HOOK UP.COM

1
ALAMO.COM

2
COWTOPIA.COM

3
THE FARMER'S MARKET.NET

4
SMALL BOOKS.COM

5
MOVING HOUSES.COM

6
SOLD OUT EVENTS

7
ACOOT

8
FLIP DOG

alamo.com

1

MovingHouses.com

5

Cowtopia.com

2

Sold Out Events.com

6

The FARMER'S MARKET .Net

3

ACOOT

7

small-books.com
We make small books for big minds

4

FlipDog™ .com

8

theproshop.com

1

CIUDAD FUTURA SM

4

versity.com

5

GlobailearningSystems.com

2

KENYABYDESIGN.COM

6

PRIME
MaineLobster

3

monster®.com

7

1
BLUE MOUNTAIN

2
PEOPLE FINDERS.COM

3
JOE FIXIT.COM

4
GOTO.COM

5
EXODUS

6
STAMPS.COM

7
FORE WARD LINKS

8
E STYLE.COM

1

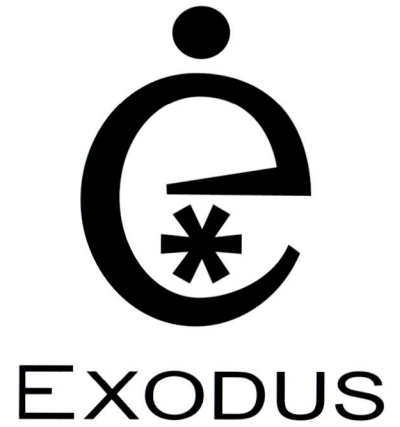

5

2

6

3

7

4

8

1

2

3

4

5

6

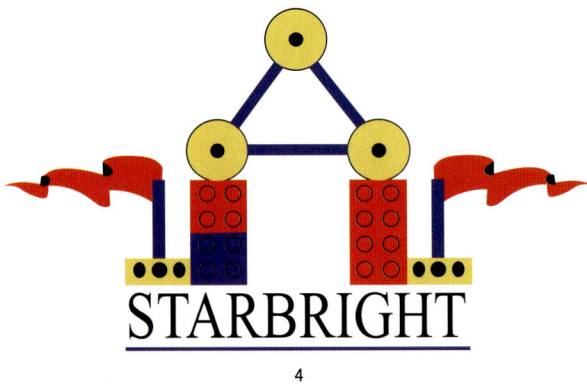

7

8

1
HEAR ME

2
INTERACTIVE FUTURES

3
ALL ADVANTAGE.COM

4
STARBRIGHT

5
AH BABY.COM

6
BRIDGE PATH.COM

7
SEARCH DATABASE.COM

8
GOV WORKS.COM

1
S & P

2
HOME BYTES.COM

3
EXTREME TIX.COM

4
FAMILY CLICK.COM

5
TRIPOD

6
G.BALL.COM

7
AWAY.COM

8
LAST MINUTE TRAVEL.COM

9
SEE U THERE

1

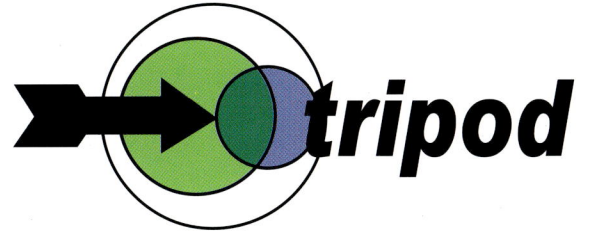

5

2

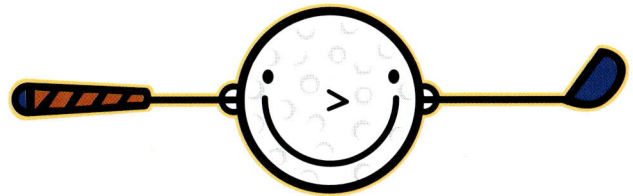

6

7

3

8

4

9

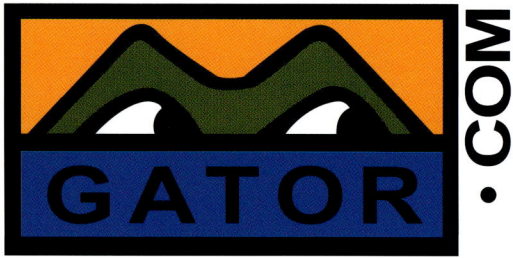

GATOR.COM

1

BET.COM

2

ALERTWIRE

3

YAHOO!

4

e21 CORP

5

QORUS.COM

6

e ™

7

RIDETHEPIPE.COM

8

1
GATOR.COM

2
BET.COM

3
ALERTWIRE

4
WWW.YAHOO.COM

5
E 21 CORP

6
QORUS.COM

7
WWW.XMLECONTENT.COM

8
RIDETHEPIPE.COM

1
LIOOS

2
ANTARA NET

3
DOMAINPEOPLE.COM

4
RIGHT POINT REAL-TIME E MAR-
KETING

5
PEOPLE.COM

6
TALK CITY

7
GO.COM

8
I WIN.COM

1

5

ANTARA.net

2

Building Communities for Business Online

6

3

7

Real-Time eMarketing

4

8

285

1

2

3

SOLUTIONS FOR eBUSINESS

4

5

6

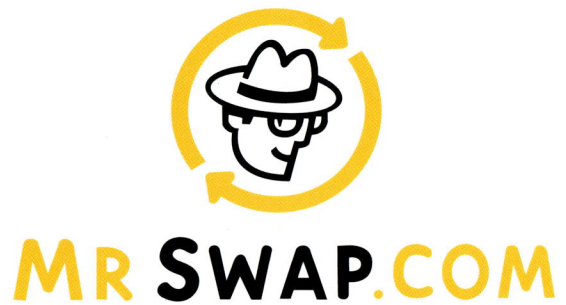

7

1
ALTA VISTA SHOPPING.COM

2
LISTEN NETWORK

3
PING NET

4
CINTRA

5
JOE EXPLORER.COM

6
AWARDS.COM

7
MR SWAP.COM

1
TELOCITY

2
LUCKY SURF.COM

3
GURU.COM

4
THE EVERYWOMAN'S COMPANY

5
SWOON

6
NETCENTIVES

7
DIAMOND.COM

8
AUTHORIA

5

1

6

2

7

3

4

8

287

StockPower ^{SM}

1

2

3

4

5

6

7

8

1
STOCK POWER

2
EDUCATION.COM

3
FREELA

4
EXP.COM

5
ESCRUBS.COM

6
SEARCH SOFTWARE AMERICA

7
DATADORK.COM

8
APARTMENT GUIDE.COM

1
SITE 59

2
FOURTH CHANNEL

3
MUSIC MAKER.COM

4
YOU DECIDE.COM

5
NEXT SET

6
SICOLA MARTIN/HANDTECH.COM

7
BRAINPOWER

1

4

the power of internet buying and selling

2

5

6

3

7

1

2

6

3

7

4

5

8

1
CLAUETA

2
BUZZSAW.COM

3
AUSTIN ATWORK.COM

4
DMIND

5
WEB MORTAR

6
ITS

7
KEEN.COM

8
GEO CITIES

1
LAKE COUNTRY BY OWNER.COM

2
PATTYSPETALS.COM

3
GAY.COM

4
LEARN IT CORP.COM

5
TICKETS.COM

6
EXCITE

7
ATHLETES VILLAGE.COM

LearnitCorp.com™

4

LakeCountry ByOwner.com ™

1

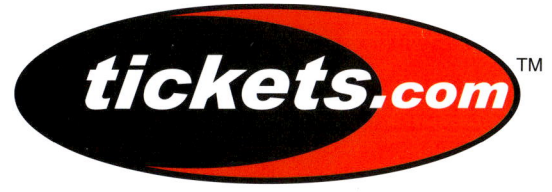

tickets.com ™

5

PattysPetals .com

2

excite

6

GAY.COM ™

3

Athletes Village . com

7

291

GeoCities

1

TechRepublic

2

eToys ®
We Bring the Toy Store to You

5

mucho.com

6

dsspro.com

3

IDI.tv

7

4

shipper.com

8

1
GEO CITIES

2
TECH REPUBLIC

3
DSSPRO.COM

4
U.S.WEB

5
ETOYS

6
MUCHO.COM

7
IDI.TV

8
SHIPPER.COM

1
L90

2
WINFIRE

3
UPROAR

4
TRAVELEZE.COM

5
INDIVIDUAL.COM

6
WORKOUT.COM

7
GO 2 MAC.COM

8
PERKS.COM

individual.com ™

5

L90

MARKETING | TECHNOLOGY | MEDIA

1

Winfire®

2

Workout.com

6

U**Pr**oar SM

3

Go 2 mac
.com

7

Traveleze**.com**

Changing the way t e world travels

4

perks.com ™

8

293

Biz**e**Port.com INC
1

desktop
news
5

1
BIZE PORT.COM INC

2
LISTEN.COM

3
BUILT 2XL

4
FOGDOG.COM

5
DESKTOP NEWS

6
THE PYTHIAN GROUP

7
FREE WORKS.COM

8
COMPUTERJOBS.COM

listen.com
Find your music
2

The Pythian Group
6

BUILT2XL
3

Freeworks
.com
7

D
F O G
G

fogdog.com
4

computerjobs.com®
8

1
GOINET

2
VALUE NET

3
COMPETE.INC

4
INTERTAINER

5
DVDJAM.COM

6
ANIMALHOUSE.COM

7
MOVIES.COM

www.goinet.com

1

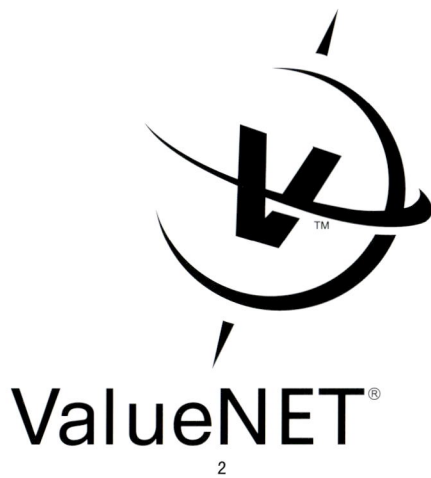

intertainer®

4

5

ValueNET®

2

animalhouse.com

6

COMPETE,INC.

3

movies.com

7

Amacis ™

1

via INMARSAT

2

Max manager ™

3

OrderFusion ™

4

Marketing World

5

UNICRU ™

6

STUDLEY

7

iwidgets

8

1
AMACIS

2
VIA INMARSAT

3
MAX MANAGER

4
ORDER FUSION

5
MARKETING WORLD

6
UNICRU

7
STUDLEY

8
IWIDGETS

1
E LINK

2
SCIENT

3
ALVARION

4
MATCHLOGIC

5
GUARDIAN UNLIMITED

6
ARIS

7
ESAVIO

8
PARLANO

1

5

6

2

3

7

4

8

NaviSote

1

Shipper
.com

5

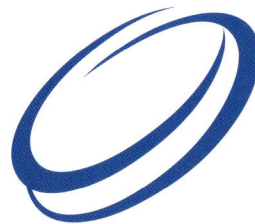

OAG

2

lasso
TECHNOLOGIES

6

Interland

3

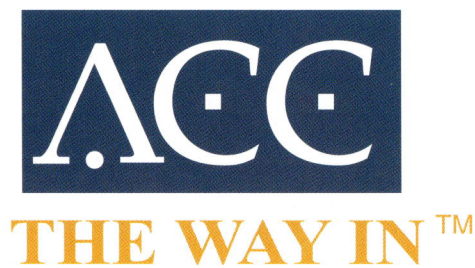

7

ACC
THE WAY IN ™

4

TouchScape

8

1
NAVI SOTE

2
OAG

3
INTERLAND

4
ACC

5
SHIPPER.COM

6
LASSO TECHNOLOGIES

7
VITRIA

8
TOUCH SCAPE

1
CORIO

2
ENSIM

3
CONVERGENCE CORRIDOR

4
FAST

5
INTELLI DYN

6
SHOW BIZ DATA

7
BEYOND.COM

8
ELECTRON ECONOMY

1

5

6

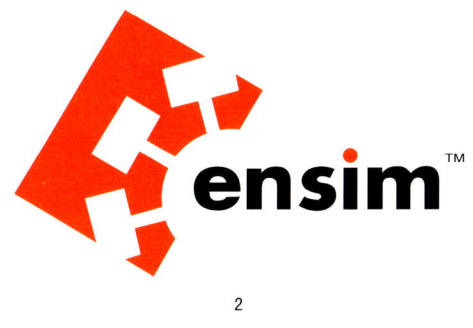

2

7

3

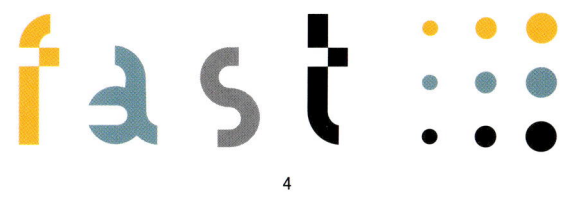

4

8

1

5

UpShot.com™

2

6

3

DIGITAL IMPACT

7

EASTBORN
SLAAPSYSTEMEN

4

8

1
NETIQ

2
UP SHOT.COM

3
TSNN.COM

4
EASTBORN SLAAPSYSTEMEN

5
ARIBA

6
DOMAIN STORE

7
DIGITAL IMPACT

8
SIWAVE

1
LAUNCH CENTER39

2
RESONATE

3
SAGEO A HEWITTE BUSINESS

4
LIVE UNIVERSE.COM

5
ADERO

6
CENTEGY

7
X CHANGE

8
CEJKA AND COMPANY

9
FIZZY LAB

1

5

2

6

3

7

4

8

9

1

CBSI

5

1
VIRYANET

2
INTRASPECT

3
VIGNETTE

4
INFOGRAMES

5
CBSI

6
EPOCH INTERNET

7
CAIS INTERNET

8
FRONTSTEP

2

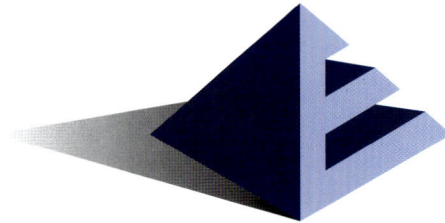

6

3

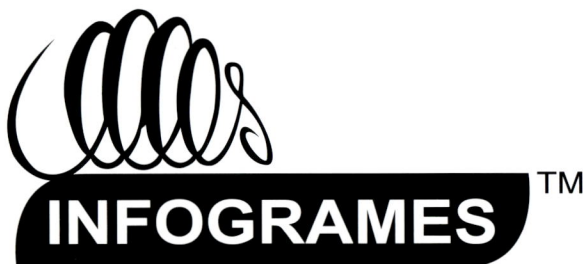

7

4

8

1
THE LTC GROUP

2
PROGRESSIVE ENTERPRIESES

3
PROGRESSIVE ENTERPRISES

4
ACTINIC

5
CLICK 2 SEND

6
KALIDO

7
PORT ERA

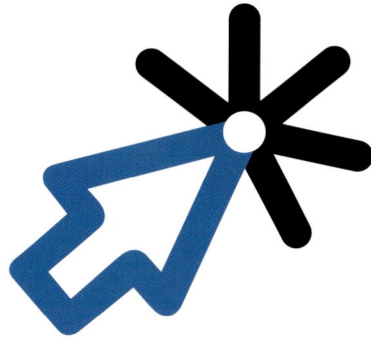

1

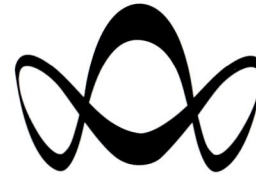

ACTINIC

4

5

2

KALIDO

6

3

PORTERA™

7

1

2

6

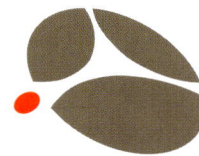

7

3

4

8

5

9

1
GO WAREHOUSE

2
3GA CORPORATION

3
E HELP

4
ENTERWORKS

5
ATLAS COMMERCE

6
VERSATA

7
INRANGE

8
THE MOMENT

9
E FAVORITES

1

6

2

7

3

8

4

9

1

5

6

2

7

3

8

4

5

1

6

2

7

3

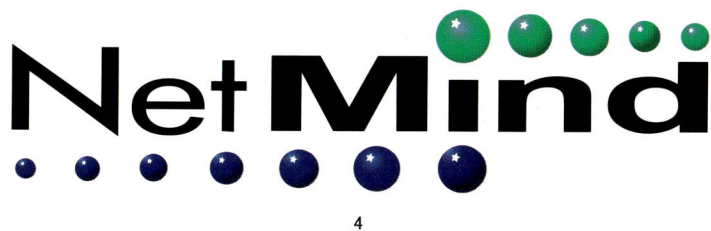

4

8

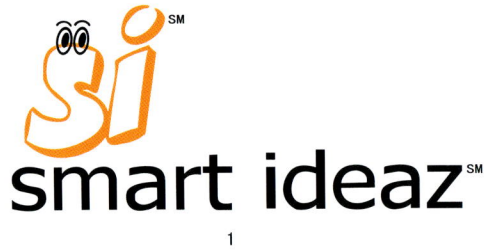

1

2

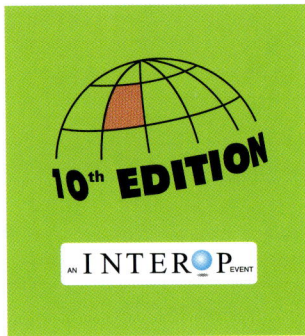

3

5

6

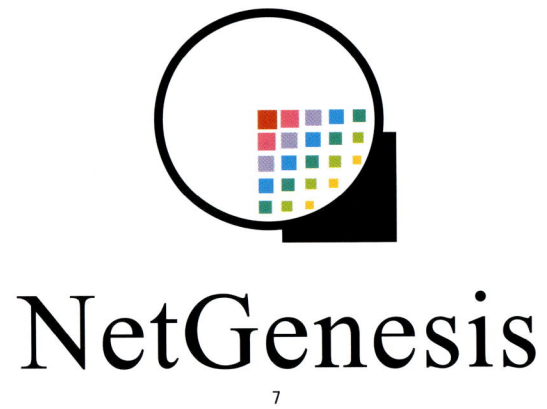

7

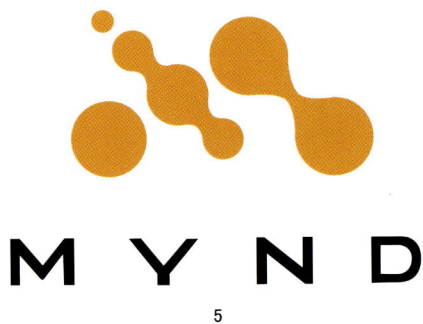

5

8

1
SMART IDEAZ

2
10ᵗ EDITION

3
BRIGHTY!

4
MYND

5
WW CHOICE

6
STENTOR

7
NET GENESIS

8
RESOURCIGENT

1
QAD

2
HABAMA

3
ARCPLAN

4
ALLEGIS

5
NETOPIA

6
CITY NET

7
IGUANA

8
ARES

4

1

5

6

2

7

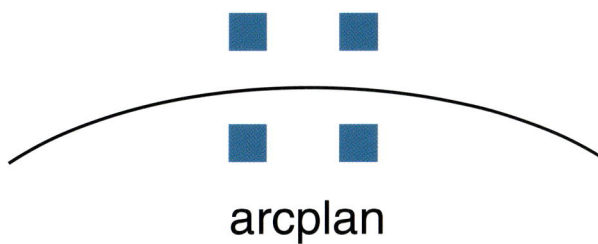

3

8

1

2

3

4

WHEELHOUSE

5

6

7

8

1
OM

2
SAS

3
SEE IT WORK.COM

4
ILUX

5
PRINCETON POWERING E BILLING
AND PAYMENTS

6
INTERACT.COM

7
INDUSTRY TO INDUSTRY

8
INTER BIZ

1

5

6

2

7

3

4

8

1

5

2

3

6

4

7

1
E BRIDGE

2
ANSWER LOGIC

3
ISYNDICATE

4
REAL CENTRIC

5
QUICK SOURCE.INC

6
EPRISE

7
VENDOR TECH

1
INSIGHT EXPRESS

2
PTC

3
CENTRA

4
ILINK GLOBAL

5
OBJECT STORM

6
NETSCOUT

7
ENERMETRIX.COM

INSIGHT EXPRESS
1

iLink
Global
4

ObjectStorm™
5

PTC
2

NetScout
6

Centra®
3

Enermetrix.com SM
Internet commerce for energy.
7

VIANT

1

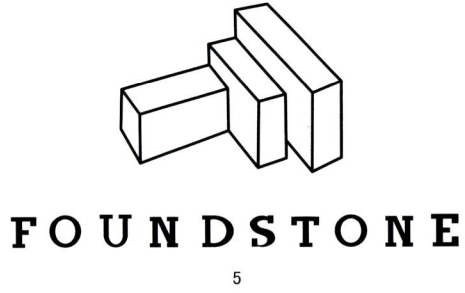

www.bolt.com

2

GoBizness ®

3

QED ™

4

FOUNDSTONE

5

eziaz SM

6

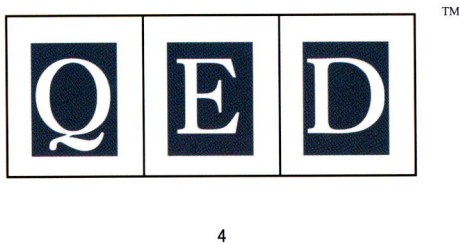

QUOTE.COM

7

mascotnetwork

8

1
VIANT

2
BOLT

3
GO BIZNESS

4
QED

5
FOUND STONE

6
E ZIAZ

7
QUOTE.COM

8
MASCOT NETWORK

INFINIUM
do great work

5

Intelsat.

1

SynQuest

6

kabl!nk

2

ventro™

7

F▲ME

3

INROADS®

4

headstrong

8

1

2

5

3

6

4

7

8

1
SAVVIS

2
PETRO COSM

3
SABA

4
RAGING KNOWLEDGE

5
EQUANT

6
VANGUARD MANAGED SOLUTIONS

7
BRUT

8
THINK LINK

1
NETFISH

2
MASTERS OF THE WEB

3
MOBIUS

4
HYPER FEED

5
STREAMSERVE

6
DST INTERNATIONAL

7
PASSPORT CORPORATION

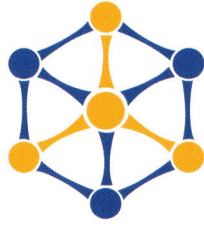

Netfish

1

HyperFeed®

4

STREAMSERVE™

5

Masters of
the Web

2

DST INTERNATIONAL

6

MOBIUS®

3

PASSPORT®
CORPORATION

7

i-Escrow®

1

5

summit strategies

2

6

PRIMARK

3

E.PIPHANY

7

KINTANA

4

eGain

8

1
I—ESCROW

2
SUMMIT STRATEGIES

3
PRIMARK

4
KINTANA

5
MY SAP.COM

6
EXPONENTS

7
E.PIPHANY

8
E GAIN

1
CAPTARIS

2
SWITCHBOARD

3
E ASSIST.COM

4
NOMINUM

5
VERITUDE

6
MIRANT

7
WWW.E COMPANY.NET

8
FAST WEB

5

1

6

2

3

7

4

8

1

2

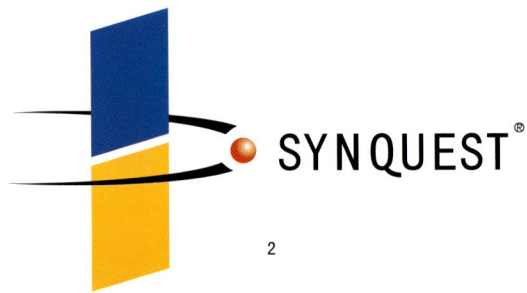

3

4

5

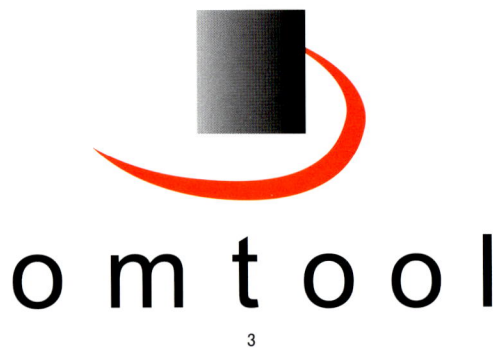